Praise for *Culinary Potions*

"Dr. Berman has done a great service for millions of people suffering from food allergies, and especially gluten intolerance. The recipes are easy to make, but more importantly they provide the foundation for a healthier life based on the food we eat."

—**Barry Sears, PhD,** author of *The Zone*

"My recipe is to take the information contained in this book and combine it with desire, intention, determination, and inspiration. Stir well and use regularly to help you create a healthier body and life."

—**Bernie Siegel, MD**
Author of *Love, Medicine & Miracles* and *Prescriptions for Living*

"Dr. Berman has created not only an informative book on food metabolism, allergies, and sensitivities, but also an enchanting collection of delicious recipes that should satisfy the palate of even the most finicky eaters. *Culinary Potions* is full of recipes for 'fun' and delicious foods, not the usual bland restrictive diet so often suggested for those who suffer from food allergies. Indulge and be healthy!"

—**Rosemary Gladstar,** herbalist and author of *The Family Herbal*

"*Culinary Potions* is outstanding—complete with menu suggestions, easy-to-follow recipes, and information for making personally beneficial dietary choices. A great find for anyone's culinary circle."

—**Bob Otolo**
Executive Chef, Founder and CEO of Gillian's Foods, Inc.

"As a gluten-intolerant person, I've had to miss many of life's treats, like sharing my godson's birthday cake and sampling a friend's favorite pie, but *Culinary Potions* has restored sweet delights to my table. Having a food allergy no longer means having to live a life of deprivation . . . and the cream puffs really *are* Dream Puffs!"

—**Evelyn C. Rysdyk**
Modern Shamanic Living

CULINARY POTIONS

Eating Joyously with Food Allergies

Wheat-Free, Potato-Free, and Corn-Free Recipes

EVE BERMAN, DO

Foreword by Christiane Northrup, MD, FACOG

Living Light Press
Cape Porpoise, Maine

Published by: Living Light Press
PO Box 7266
Cape Porpoise, ME 04014
www.culinarypotions.com

Editor: Ellen Kleiner
Book design and production: Janice St. Marie
Cover and interior art: Olga Pastuchiv

The information and recommendations in this book are based on the author's clinical practice and are not meant to replace medical advice. Readers are advised to follow their physician's recommendations to ensure that individualized nutritional needs are met.

Printed in the United States of America on acid-free recycled paper

Publisher's Cataloging-in-Publication Data

Berman, Eve.
    Culinary potions : eating joyously with food
allergies : wheat-free, potato-free, and corn-free
recipes / by Eve Berman ; foreword by Christiane
Northrup. — 1st ed.

        p. cm.
        LCCN: 2001126189
        ISBN: 0-9708374-0-2

    1. Food allergy—Diet therapy—Recipes.   I. Title.

RC588.D53B47 2001   641.5'631
                                     QBI01-200909

10 9 8 7 6 5 4 3 2 1

To my wondrous patients . . .
who inspired me to write this book
and keep the magic brewing
so that others might reclaim their health

In gratitude . . .

An at-home cook struggling with food sensitivities relies on many sources for ideas and assistance. I especially wish to thank all the chefs whose dishes propelled me into the kitchen to recreate flavors and textures in a form suitable for people with food allergies.

I am filled with gratitude to Ellen Kleiner of Blessingway Authors' Services for midwifing this book; holding to an objective, professional standard; and offering playful encouragement and guidance along the way.

Evie, you are an awesome art director and visionary. I needed all the love, brainstorming sessions, second opinions, and hand-holding you provided.

Olga, your artwork is luscious and always a joy to behold.

Dave, you do help people's dreams come true! Thanks for believing in this project. I couldn't have survived the computer without your knowledge, support, and patience for working with the technology challenged.

Claudia, you have always encouraged me on whatever path I take. Thanks for testing the recipes.

Aliyah, you have the most exemplary palate. Thanks for all the fine-tuning, recommendations, and motivation to concoct anew.

Joseph, for forever encouraging me to fulfill my soul's purpose and for eating all the mistakes, I thank you.

CONTENTS

DESSERTS

APPENDIXES

FOREWORD

For hundreds of thousands of years, human food has come fresh from the land or sea and been eaten whole and unprocessed, other than when it's been first cooked, or preserved through natural salting, drying, or freezing methods. This is the type of diet our digestive systems were designed to handle. In addition, because humans coevolved with a wide variety of plants and animals, our digestive systems have come to rely on a great diversity of nutrients.

Over the last eighty years, however, the human food supply has changed dramatically—more than in all other historical eras combined. These eight decades have given rise to additives, such as monosodium glutamate (MSG) and food coloring; processed and refined foods, stripped of many health-promoting nutrients; and fake fats, such as margarine and shortening, made from partially hydrogenated oils. But our bodies were not designed to assimilate such devitalized substances.

Also in recent decades, agricultural monoculture has nearly eliminated the availability of genetically diverse plant and animal nutrients. Today, agribusiness uses relatively few high-yield plant and animal species to produce the foods we most commonly eat. For example, wheat that is grown for the production of flour comes from a scant number of seed types, whereas wheat grown naturally varies greatly from place to place, even within the same field, and is not subject to the alterations induced by chemical fertilizers and pesticides. Likewise, the potatoes and corn we eat are undiversified and at times entirely altered. This means that we consume the same types of food proteins, carbohydrates, and fats over and over again, with little of the variation required for optimal health.

These and other changes in the food supply contribute to diets that deviate radically from the mixture of micronutrients and macronutrients our bodies were meant to metabolize. As a result, food allergies and sensitivities are more common now than ever before, as are food-related disorders such as obesity and heart disease.

So how does one stay healthy? If you experience fatigue, digestive problems, or other symptoms of food allergy, do you have to drop out of society and give up your favorite foods, or live in a monastery bordered by an organic garden? Hardly. Despite our Stone Age metabolism, we humans are very adaptable. With a few adjustments, including elimination of the most pesky culprits, it's possible to feel healthier and more productive than ever before.

This is where *Culinary Potions* comes in. This cookbook and nutritional guide by Dr. Eve Berman, a physician and colleague I've known for many years, is filled with tried-and-true tips and recipes for eating well while treating food allergy. One glance at the chocolate desserts listed in the table of contents will tell you it does not advocate a healing-through-deprivation approach. Dr. Berman knows from both personal and professional experience that dietary deprivation ultimately leads not to health but to addictive, out-of-control eating. And so this book offers helpful, friendly, and practical advice on shifting from dietary deprivation to dietary improvement—eating for health and pleasure.

In over twenty years of clinical practice, I have found that dietary improvement is one of the fastest, most reliable ways to eradicate symptoms ranging from painful joints to insomnia. Whatever your symptoms are, *Culinary Potions* will get you started and keep you going in a healthier direction. Believe me, treating food allergy never tasted so good!

—Christiane Northrup, MD, FACOG
Author of *Women's Bodies, Women's Wisdom* and *The Wisdom of Menopause*

PREFACE

The purpose of this book is to provide a foundation of information and recipes so people can create healthy meals that incorporate fun foods without the ingredients that trigger sensitivities or allergies. The concept of *Culinary Potions* was born while I was consulting with a patient, jotting down notes on scraps of paper for her to take home, as I had done numerous times before, all the while knowing she would undoubtedly call me back to clarify the information. I realized then how helpful it might be to write a book that combined nutritional information I had gathered in clinical practice as an osteopathic physician with recipes I had created to fulfill my personal need for enjoyable and nutritious meals.

I began my own process of healing as a seventeen-year-old college student. At the time, I was constantly tired—a condition that had started in the eighth grade when I was out of school for a month with fatigue and severe episodic stomach cramps. Although doctors thought I might have mononucleosis, this hunch was never substantiated by blood tests, and I now believe I was suffering from micromercurialism, a mild form of mercury poisoning. The fatigue that resurfaced in my college years seemed to have multiple causes.

Before long I found that at any given meal, I needed protein and could eat only small amounts of sugar and fat. As my healing progressed, I discovered that the right nourishment was a significant factor in getting and staying well. However, I loved to eat good food prepared with love. So to avoid feeling deprived by eliminating the ingredients I could not tolerate, I created sumptuous recipes that nourished my body and my soul. In the process—a mission that has lasted twenty-five years—I have learned that consuming the proper balance of nutrients we need to grow physically, emotionally, intellectually, and spiritually will usually make us feel full.

For the past eleven years I have been a practicing osteopathic physician in southern Maine. Osteopathy is based on the principle that the body has inherent mechanisms for healing and is endowed with a divine blueprint that provides a map for its development and self-correction. Using palpation, a trained osteopath listens to the body's divine intelligence and assists it. Basing diagnoses and treatments on "the physician within" a patient's body allows osteopathic physicians to help many people who have not been aided by other forms of Western medicine.

In addition to my private practice, I train student physicians in Traditional Osteopathy at my office and at the University of New England College of Osteopathic Medicine, where I too attended medical school and through which I completed my postgraduate training. As an osteopath educated in the United States, I am trained not only in osteopathic medicine but also in allopathic medicine, as well as being licensed to prescribe pharmaceuticals and perform surgery. I utilize blood work, medical history, and physical exams to assist in developing a complete picture of an individual's needs and to help guide their healing. Moreover, I have been trained in a number of complementary modalities, including counseling, homeopathy, use of herbal medicines, applications of kinesiology, shamanic healing practices, and nutrition. Among these, nutrition is most fundamental to well-being and something we ourselves can focus on, giving our bodies the building blocks needed to heal and evolve.

Consequently, I often recommend alterations in diet, helping my patients reevaluate their food choices and regard food as medicine with profound effects on their physiology and overall well-being. These recommendations have benefited hundreds of adults diagnosed with allergies, chronic fatigue syndrome, fibromyalgia, osteoarthritis, rheumatoid arthritis, colitis, Crohn's disease, obesity, thyroid dysfunction, hypertension, diabetes, cardiovascular disease, and various skin conditions, as well as children with allergies, asthma, attention deficit disorder (ADD), attention deficit hyperactivity disorder (ADHD), and recurrent infections such as tonsillitis and otitis media. It is my hope that this book will similarly contribute to the healing of many individuals who suffer from these conditions.

THE ALLERGY CONNECTION

The recipes in this book are for people of all ages who cannot tolerate wheat, potatoes, or corn—the culprits responsible for most food sensitivties and allergies. Nearly all are also free of yeast and gluten, other common offenders. Dairy products and eggs are sometimes viewed as triggers too, but I have found the problems associated with them are usually caused by antibiotics, hormones, and pesticides that are fed to animals and then passed on in the food supply. It is therefore important to use *organic* dairy products and eggs in dishes that call for these ingredients.

The comfort foods described here play a valuable role in maintaining individualized diets. Most people who are restricted from eating wheat, potatoes, and corn feel deprived, and as a result are unable to remain on their food plan. The dishes in *Culinary Potions,* however, can satisfy such cravings and thus keep people on track. These fun foods can also be spirited off to parties, where no one will suspect, either by taste, consistency, or flavor, that there is anything "different" about them. Many travel well in lunch boxes too, offering an alternative to the nutrient-deficient foods served at most school lunch counters, in addition to eliminating the ingredients children are most sensitive to.

While on their own these recipes promise culinary gratification, balanced with other fare they encourage a healthy response to food by adhering to recommended protein/carbohydrate/fat (P/C/F) ratios—a method of food combining based on Dr. Barry Sears's research and referred to as Zone nutrition. The ratios, listed in grams for each recipe, assist in creating balanced meals that regulate the physiologic response to food. Further, they help in assessing the true content of portions of any size, thus providing the knowledge needed to take personal responsibility for nourishment.

To prepare a balanced meal, choose a carbohydrate first and add protein and fat to go with it. For example: you want Wiffle Waffles (see page 35) for breakfast. We know that 1 waffle contains the following ratio of nutrients:

	P	C	F
1 Wiffle Waffle	7	23	10
Add protein:			
2 egg whites with mushrooms	14		
Add a drizzle of maple syrup		4	
Totals	21	27	10

Another example: you have just baked Daybreak Bars (see page 97) and want some for dessert.

	P	C	F
1$^1/_2$ Daybreak Bars	3	20	10
Add protein:			
2 ounces of steak	18		5
Add a small salad		5	
Totals	21	25	15

These two examples are based on guidelines for a person who needs approximately 20 grams of protein per meal, or 60 to 80 grams of protein per day. (See "Guidelines for a Balanced Diet," on page 25, to estimate your daily requirements.)

Ideally, food should be selected according to these basic guidelines and modified in keeping with activity levels. As you increase activity, the overall ratios should stay the same but the amount of food per meal, and possibly the number of meals per day, should increase. Because you are a living organism, growing and changing emotionally and spiritually as well as physically, it may be necessary to adjust your food selections and quantities slightly from day to day, week to week, or season to season. For a more individualized estimate based on percent of body fat, lean muscle mass, and activity level, refer to Dr. Sears's books listed on page 135.

For most desserts in this book, all you need to fill your carbohydrate requirement per meal is one serving. In some instances it may be best to eat only one serving *per day*, reducing your consumption of granulated sugar and chocolate. If you tend to overeat or suffer from food addictions, even this much sugar and chocolate may be intolerable, due to its stimulating effect on compulsive behavior.

Because some types of carbohydrates can radically increase blood sugar levels, it is a good idea to limit carbohydrate choices to foods low on the glycemic index (see Appendix C for guidance). Safe options are rice, other easy-to-tolerate grains, as well as fruits and vegetables. The recipes in this book for breads, crepes, and pizza crust are all acceptable. A single serving per meal is recommended, and it is helpful to vary selections from one meal to the next. If you can tolerate sugar, sample carbohydrate choices to enjoy with protein over the course of a day might be the following: for one meal, sandwich bread; for a second meal, rice or a piece of fruit; and for a third meal, a cookie. Adding two snacks of a half portion of fruit, a half portion of grain, or a half portion of bread provides enough calories per day.

To round out your diet nutritionally, add a side dish of steamed vegetables or a salad, and also good fats (see page 23). Avoid root and similarly high-glycemic index vegetables, such as winter squash, parsnips, turnips, and corn. Other vegetables contain insignificant amounts of carbohydrates and thus do not need to be calculated in total ratios. To enhance the vitamin and mineral content of meals, add seaweed or other sea vegetables.

An additional facet of nutrition to consider is salt, the unfortunate victim of a bad rap. When medical studies showed that salt raises blood pressure, people began restricting their salt intake whether they had hypertension or not. Many of my patients with chronic fatigue syndrome and fibromyalgia have low blood pressure and are deficient in salt. If you have low or normal blood pressure, salt your food; this will lessen your fatigue and enhance your physical, emotional, and spiritual well-being. As for brands, I recommend Celtic Sea Salt, because it contains both macro and trace minerals, does not contribute to water retention, and tastes exceptionally good. Whereas I dislike ordinary table salt, I will lick Celtic Sea Salt off a spoon. Most health food stores stock this organic ingredient; those that don't may be willing to order it for you (see Appendix A for a reliable source). If you have an aversion to salt, you may have a salt deficiency. If you crave salt, you probably need it. Salt pills and spoonfuls of salt are ill-advised unless a physician is monitoring your blood. Instead, salting your food to taste is the best way to have it boost your energy.

It is possible to fully recover from some food allergies, but this requires time and a firm commitment to healing. Although recovery programs are beyond the scope of this book, the initial steps are outlined here: avoiding foods you are sensitive or allergic to, regarding food as medicine that modulates your physiologic responses, consuming toxin-free ingredients, and eating meals that nourish your soul.

BALANCING PROTEINS,
CARBOHYDRATES, AND FATS

Altering the balance of proteins, carbohydrates, and fats changes the body's physiological response to food. Without such adjustments the body is apt to produce an increase in allergic reactions, as well as inflammation (swelling), vasoconstriction (narrowing of the blood vessels), cellular proliferation (growths), and a host of other unwanted effects.

Specifically, overly low protein-to-carbohydrate ratios can increase insulin concentrations, leading to unstable blood sugars; decrease glucagon concentrations, contributing to excessive storage of sugars and fats; escalate the production of hormones that promote inflammation, vasoconstriction, cellular proliferation, and platelet aggregation (clotting); and depress the immune response. Conditions with a large inflammatory component include osteoarthritis, rheumatoid arthritis, some symptoms of premenstrual syndrome (PMS), colitis, Crohn's disease, asthma, fibromyalgia, candidiasis, and myalgias (muscle pains). Vasoconstriction contributes to hypertension and bronchospasm. Clotting can result in exacerbations of peripheral vascular disease, stroke, and heart attack. A depressed immune response manifests in such recurrent infections as tonsillitis, otitis media, viral illness, and yeast and fungal disorders. Some symptoms of ADD and ADHD are due to food allergies, and exacerbations correlate with the ingestion of these foods or unstable blood sugar levels, usually following overly low protein-to-carbohydrate meals.

The goal to strive for is meals composed of appropriate amounts of food—no more than 500 calories—in balanced proportions. This way you will not only maintain or regain your health but also provide your body with the fuel it needs to run efficiently. Simultaneously your body type may shift. If you are of normal weight that is effectively distributed between lean muscle mass and fat, your body type will remain the same. But if you have a high percentage of body fat, you will burn off the excess and increase your lean muscle mass. And if you have a normal percentage of body fat but insufficient muscle mass, you can increase your muscle mass if you so desire. The following descriptions of the essential building blocks of healthy eating derive from years of experimenting on myself and helping patients achieve a relationship with food that supports well-being on all levels.

Proteins

Proteins stimulate glucagon excretion, which in turn mobilizes the metabolism of stored sugars and fats into energy. Proteins also build and maintain muscle mass and help ground the energy system. However, many people are apprehensive because of literature warning that too much protein may exacerbate osteoporosis and kidney disease. While this is true, it must be determined how much is too much for any individual. In my practice I utilize blood work, medical history, and physical exams to evaluate approp-riate amounts and proportions when designing a specialized food plan.

Regarding daily requirements of protein, a sedentary person 5 feet to 5 feet 7 inches tall typically needs 60 to 80 grams of protein per day (20 to 27 grams per meal). A person 5 feet 8 inches to 6 feet tall needs 90 to 110 grams per day (30 to 37 grams per meal). More active individuals require increased amounts of protein. If you eat snacks in addition to three meals a day, adjust your per-meal requirements accordingly.

Good sources of protein are lean beef, chicken, pork, turkey, and fish. Other usually reliable sources are the following:

Tofu. Some people assimilate soy/vegetable protein well, whereas others do not. A meal composed of 25 grams of tofu would require approximately $1/2$ a square in a prepackaged tub. If your only source of protein that day were tofu, you would need to consume $1^1/_2$ to 2 tubs over the twenty-four-hour period. *The Soy Zone* by Dr. Sears contains good examples of balanced meals incorporating soy. Be advised that tofu and other soy/vegetable protein foods also contain carbohydrates—a factor to take into account when calculating P/C/F ratios. Remember, too, that the health benefits of soy are still under investigation despite its recent popularity.

Complementary proteins. It is possible to rely on complementary proteins like rice and beans as long as you add extra protein to balance out the carbohydrates in these foods. Most vegetarians use textured veg-etable protein (TVP) for this purpose. When planning a complementary protein meal, remember that if you are sensitive to potatoes and corn you may also be sensitive to many beans.

Eggs and dairy products. Eggs are an easy source of protein. Cottage cheese and yogurt can also be used as a complete protein source, but you will need to take their carbohydrate and fat content into account while building a balanced meal. Cheeses can be used as well, but most are high in fat. If you get stomachaches or gain weight easily from too much fat, save cheese for a snack or condiment rather than the main protein source of a meal (see Appendix B for amounts of fat and protein in dairy items).

Protein powder. For a balanced meal, sprinkle a carbohydrate-free protein powder over a stir fry, or mix it with oatmeal or a shake.

Nuts. Although nuts are a good source of protein, they contain a lot of fat and should, like cheese, be eaten as a snack or condiment rather than as a main protein source. Moreover, peanut butter has been found to contain funguses that are best avoided by some individuals. A good substitute is almond butter, which has a greater protein-to-carbohydrate ratio.

When specifying sources of protein, I recommend organic meats, organic eggs and dairy products, and farm-raised fish because these contain few or no pesticides, herbicides, hormones, antibiotics, toxic metals, or other known toxins. Most people with allergies, chronic fatigue syndrome, fibromyalgia, or inflammatory-based disease are sensitive to toxins in their food and should therefore avoid them.

Carbohydrates

Carbohydrates are starches found primarily in pastas, breads, fruits, and vegetables. Broken down in the body, they become sugars that can be either used or stored. If you eat too many carbohydrates, they will be stored as fat, increasing your percentage of body fat.

Some carbohydrates are rapidly absorbed, contributing to quickly skyrocketing blood sugar levels. Foods with a high glycemic index (see Appendix C) are most likely to produce this sugar "high," which is similar in effect to eating a candy bar. However, just as quickly your blood sugar level will plummet, leading to a sugar "low." While tired, you may crave more carbohydrates to regain your energy, resulting in a Ping-Pong effect that throws the body out of balance and causes periods of fatigue throughout the day.

Another result of ingesting too many carbohydrates is the excessive formation of powerful hormones from fatty acid metabolism. These hormones, known as eicosanoids, increase allergic sensitivity, inflammation, vaso-constriction, cellular proliferation, and clotting, while decreasing the immune response. If you have allergies, chronic fatigue syndrome, or inflammatory-based disease, be sure to eat the right amount of carbohydrate, as indicated below.

For many individuals with these conditions the *type* of carbohydrate is also problematic. Most are extremely sensitive to wheat, potatoes, and corn. Some cannot tolerate the gluten in wheat; others have difficulty with the rancid oils in refined flours. In the first stages of healing, it is not necessary to know the reason for your sensitivities but rather to determine whether you are sensitive. Signs of sensitivity include nausea, indigestion, diarrhea, fatigue, itchy skin, rashes, headaches, muscle weakness, swollen and stiff joints, breathing difficulty, and tinnitus. Once you have con-cluded that you are suffering from food allergies, eliminate from your diet all potentially problematic foods—such as wheat, potatoes, corn, refined sugars, nonorganic dairy products, fermented foods, and yeasts—until you feel better, then reintroduce them one at a time in small amounts to discover those that are causing your symptoms. Types of carbohydrate that can be tolerated differ from one person to another. For example, whereas some people are able to eat potatoes but not corn or wheat, others can tol-erate corn but not potatoes.

This elimination experiment offers additional benefits, stabilizing blood sugar levels and ridding the body of excess yeasts by cutting off their food supply, which is primarily sugars. Since many people with allergies, chronic fatigue syndrome, fibromyalgia, or inflammatory-based disease have an overgrowth of yeast, its elimination is imperative for other healing to take place.

Regarding daily requirements of carbohydrates, a person 5 feet to 5 feet 7 inches tall typically needs 80 to 100 grams per day (20 to 33 grams per meal), which is the equivalent of $1/_2$ cup of rice or an apple. A person 5 feet 8 inches to 6 feet tall needs 120 to 145 grams per day (40 to 48 grams per meal). If you eat snacks in addition to three meals a day, adjust your per-meal requirements accordingly. For optimal sugar control, eat low-glycemic index foods.

Fats

Believe it or not, fats are important for balanced nutrition. They provide the primary fuel for muscles at rest, help form the cell membranes, and are the building blocks for hormones. As a result, a low-fat or no-fat diet can actually make people fat and ill. Moreover, since fats help us feel full, consumption of the proper type and amount staves off feelings of deprivation and promotes maintenance of a healthy diet. For individuals who are of normal weight or underweight, or who are high-performance athletes, fats are also a good way to add calories.

Generally, saturated fats found in butter, dairy, coconut oil, palm kernel oil, and lean meat are good choices, as are monounsaturated fats from peanut oil, olive oil, sesame oil, avocado, sesame tahini, and nuts. Essential fatty acids, required for normal functioning, must be eaten since our bodies cannot produce them. These beneficial polyunsaturated fats are found in such oils as unrefined and properly stored flaxseed, walnut, borage, primrose, and olive. Healthy fats are also found in oatmeal, which is highly recommended for gluten-tolerant individuals. Fats from fish sources are likewise advantageous provided they are free of heavy metals, dioxin, and other chemical toxins from polluted waterways. To research the toxins in your local rivers, streams, and lakes, contact your state's Fish and Game Department.

In contrast to beneficial fats, oils with unstable chemical structures are not as good for you. Oils that have been processed by hydrogenation are chemically changed and contain trans-fatty acids that have deleterious effects on the body's biochemistry. Those most often found in processed foods are corn, canola, soybean, safflower, and sunflower oils. When stored improperly, any oil with an unstable chemical structure bonds easily to oxygen, by exposure either to air or to excess free radicals in the body, causing the formation of toxins, including carcinogens. Most heated oils too can contribute to the formation of toxins and excess free radicals. Foods sautéed at a low heat are fine, and fried foods in moderation will not harm you. The best oils for sautéing and deep-frying are coconut, peanut, sesame, and olive. In her book *Know Your Fats*, Mary Enig, PhD, recommends a blend of $1/3$ coconut, $1/3$ sesame, and $1/3$ olive oils for all-purpose frying. In this book, I have listed coconut oil in the few recipes for fried foods, such as Chicken Charms (see page 69) and Abracadabra Citrus Beef (see page 75), but you can substitute Dr. Enig's blend if you prefer.

Regarding daily requirements of fat, a person 5 feet to 5 feet 7 inches tall typically needs approximately 30 to 40 grams of fat per day (10 to 20 grams per meal). A person 5 feet 8 inches to 6 feet tall needs approximately 45 to 55 grams of fat per day (15 to 18 grams per meal). If you eat snacks in addition to three meals a day, adjust your per-meal requirements accordingly.

Most people have no difficulty getting enough fats. If you eat meat or fish, you may not have to think about adding fats because you get them with your protein. To increase your consumption of good fats, drink milk, eat oats if you are gluten tolerant, butter your bread, bake with butter or coconut oil, and drizzle homemade dressings or mayonnaise (see pages 49–51) on your salads. However, if you are vegetarian, monitor your fat intake daily to be sure you are getting enough.

GUIDELINES FOR A BALANCED DIET

☆ Eat approximately every 4 to 6 hours. If more time elapses between meals, have a snack.

☆ Avoid overeating. In general, consume no more than 500 calories at any meal.

☆ Salt food to taste.

☆ At each meal eat protein, carbohydrates, and fats in recommended proportions. If you exercise daily or are a high-performance athlete, eat more food in the same proportions, adding extra calories by increasing your intake of fats.

Daily Requirements of Proteins, Carbohydrates, and Fats

For people 5 feet to 5 feet 7 inches tall—60 to 80 grams of protein, 80 to 100 grams of carbohydrates, and 30 to 40 grams of fat

For people 5 feet 8 inches to 6 feet tall—90 to 110 grams of protein, 120 to 145 grams of carbohydrates, and 45 to 55 grams of fat

For more detailed estimates, see Dr. Sears's books listed on page 135.

Helpful Equipment

Grater

When selecting a grater, find one that is easy to clean and has interchangeable parts for grating everything from herbs and cheese to chocolate. Zyliss makes a grater with a coarse drum accessory that works well for grating chocolate.

Electric Mixer

While shopping for an electric mixer, look for one with a bread hook attachment and a setting that allows it to swing back and forth from the center to the sides of the bowl. If you find heavy mixers cumbersome, choose one that is lightweight and small enough to store easily.

Nonaluminum Cookware

To reduce your exposure to toxic metals and chemicals, avoid cooking with aluminum equipment. Use a magnet to determine whether cookware contains aluminum, even taking it along with you to stores. If the magnet adheres to a pan or utensil, it is not aluminum and can be used safely. Further, it is wise to steer clear of cookware with nonstick coatings because these materials tend to restrict the activity of the body's self-correcting mechanism, reducing health and energy levels. Cast iron equipment is usually okay, although some people are sensitive to it. Stainless steel is the best.

Salt Grinder

Most salt grinders, while capable of pulverizing other coarse sea salts, do not work well with wet Celtic Sea Salt. However, The Salt and Grain Society sells a grinder from Denmark that does (see Appendix A). To grind large amounts for baking, I also use a ceramic mortar and pestle.

Scale

Most Americans overeat, unaware of the excessive amounts of food they consume. For example, a standard restaurant serving of salmon is usually two or three meals' worth of protein for a person 5 feet to 5 feet 7 inches tall, and it is often accompanied by an appetizer, bread, and dessert. Accustomed to overly large portion sizes, when I first used a scale to gauge the weight of a steak I had estimated at 2 ounces, I was amazed to discover it weighed 4 ounces. To keep your measurements accurate, use a digital scale calibrated in grams and ounces.

Water Filter

If you cook with town or city water, invest in a filter that takes out all chemicals and bacteria. If you have a well, test your water and make sure it is free of bacteria, parasites, and excessive amounts of potentially harmful minerals, including iron.

USING THE RECIPES

The following recipes made without wheat, potatoes, or corn, and most without yeast or gluten, provide people who cannot eat such ingredients with delicious alternatives to satisfy cravings and stay on a healthy and nutritious food plan. Individuals without food allergies also enjoy them. Each dish has passed a "taste test" with children as well as adults, and all are easy to prepare, including the most exotic of them.

The recipes are divided into four sections: Breads; Soups, Dressings, and Sauces; Entrées; and Desserts. The breads are classics, selected to gratify basic needs that often go unaddressed, even in health food stores. Parents will find enough variety to keep their children's lunch boxes humming with sandwiches and snacks, and the table resplendent with waffles at Sunday brunch. The soups, dressings, and sauces present tasty solutions to other quandaries. Presto Pesto (see page 53) helps bind heavy metals accumulated primarily through exposure to dental amalgams, and Sandwich Salve (see page 51) guarantees a mayonnaise made with beneficial fats. The entrées feature a cornucopia of protein-based delights, including a breakfast hash, vegetable dishes, and selections with shrimp, chicken, or steak. Most enchanting, perhaps, is the assortment of Fairy Rings (see pages 61–66), or pizza—the pleasure food most missed by people with allergies.

The desserts offer especially sumptuous treats that keep people on a restricted diet from feeling deprived, encouraging them to refrain from eating forbidden foods. Although the dessert recipes tend to be higher in fat than is usually recommended, this should not pose a problem as long as you don't add excessive amounts of fat to other foods at the same meal, such as half a stick of butter on steamed vegetables. Individuals who are vigilant about fats can indulge safely in Daybreak Bars (see page 97) and Hidden Treasure (see page 114).

Recipe ingredients in each section of the book have been chosen for their health-promoting benefits. The dairy products and eggs used here are organic, as are all the foods I recommend, because they contain no antibiotics, hormones, or pesticides.

To accommodate individual sensitivities, most ingredients can be substituted. For example, many recipes call for milk, butter, and soy flour. Individuals who react poorly to cow's milk may substitute equal amounts of rice milk or soy milk. Butter can be replaced with equal amounts of coconut oil, which at room temperature is a solid. (Coconut oil is listed in the few recipes for fried foods, but it is possible to substitute Dr. Mary Enig's blend of $1/3$ coconut oil, $1/3$ sesame oil, and $1/3$ olive oil.) In lieu of soy flour, use equal amounts of oat flour if you can tolerate gluten, or $1/2$ tapioca flour and $1/2$ rice flour if you cannot.

A common ingredient in the dessert recipes is baking powder, which usually contains cornstarch. People who cannot tolerate the small amount of corn in baking powder may substitute $1/3$ teaspoon of baking soda plus $1/2$ teaspoon of cream of tartar for each teaspoon of baking powder.

Other potential offenders in the dessert recipes, and the bread recipes as well, are cane sugars, both granulated and brown. For every cup of sugar, you can substitute $1/2$ cup of corn-free fructose and 1 to 3 tablespoons of water. The end product will be drier but still delicious, and the yield will be reduced by 20 percent. To calculate the adjusted carbohydrate content for these recipes, subtract 150 grams for each cup of granulated sugar that is replaced, and for each cup of replaced brown sugar subtract 109 grams.

All ingredients used in the recipes are readily available. Whatever cannot be found locally may be ordered from sources listed at the back of the book (see Appendix A). Substitution is another option, especially for micronutrients. For instance, a dough recipe calling for xanthum gum can instead be made with guar gum, which is more affordable as well as easier to find on grocery store shelves.

Further, every recipe in this book includes a listing in grams of each ingredient's protein, carbohydrate, and fat content, together with total counts for the entire recipe and for individual portions. These at-a-glance calculations of macronutrients are provided to free up your energy for blending and brewing.

Let the magic begin . . .

BREADS

GRIFFINMILK BISCUITS

Yield: 18 biscuits

According to an ancient tale, a griffin bestowed gifts of golden eggs filled with griffinmilk upon a girl who, despite her fear of this creature that was part eagle and part lion, gazed at it and saw its glory. These biscuits will fill you with that fortitude and grace.

	P	C	F
1 tablespoon sugar		16	
3 tablespoons coconut oil			42
1 egg	7		7
$^1/_2$ cup rice flour	5	60	
$^1/_3$ cup tapioca flour		11	
2 teaspoons baking powder			
$^1/_2$ teaspoon baking soda			
$^1/_2$ teaspoon salt			
$1^1/_4$ tablespoons buttermilk blend powder		3	8
$^1/_3$ cup water			
Total for 18 biscuits	12	90	57
Total per biscuit		5	3

☆ Preheat the oven to 400 degrees.

☆ Mix together the sugar, coconut oil (a solid at room temperature), and egg.

☆ In a separate bowl mix together the remaining dry ingredients, then add the water and blend.

(cont.)

☆ Blend this mixture into the sugar and oil mixture.

☆ Pour the batter into a greased muffin pan, filling each cup approximately $1/2$ full.

☆ Bake for 10 to 12 minutes, checking the biscuits after about 6 minutes to make sure they are not getting too brown on top. If they are, cover them with tinfoil.

Hint: In lieu of the buttermilk blend powder, you can use $1/3$ cup of buttermilk and $1/3$ of cup water. In either case, store the baked muffins tightly covered to ensure moistness.

WIFFLE WAFFLES

Yield: 8 waffles

For two years my daughter asked me to buy a waffle iron. Finally I embarked on a quest for the perfect one and created the recipe for these tasty waffles, which are simpler and less messy than other wheatless varieties. In addition to serving them for breakfast, you can use them as sandwich bread for peanut butter and jelly, tuna, roast beef, or any other desired filling.

	P	C	F
1 cup rice flour	11	120	2
1/2 cup soy flour	40	36	22
1/2 cup tapioca flour		16	
1/2 teaspoon salt			
5 teaspoons baking powder			
1 tablespoon sugar		12	
3 eggs	21		21
1 1/2 cups 2 percent milk	12	18	6
1/4 cup olive oil			42
Total for 8 waffles	84	202	93
Total per waffle	10	25	11

☆ Preheat the waffle iron.
☆ In a large bowl, blend the flours, salt, baking powder, and sugar.
☆ Beat in the eggs and milk.
☆ Blend in the oil.
☆ Grease the waffle iron with butter.
☆ Pour on a full ladle of batter.
☆ Cook until the waffle is the desired crispness. Repeat with the remaining batter, rebuttering the waffle iron as necessary.

STICKY SWEET SWIRLY BUNS
WITH GLUTEN

Yield: 16 buns

Although I don't miss many baked goods, I do miss good cinnamon buns—small galaxies swirling with exotic spices and a sweet, buttery flavor. For various galactic needs, try these heavenly look-alikes, two with yeast and one without. However, without wheat gluten they will not be chewy and flaky.

	P	C	F
Dough:			
4 tablespoons butter			44
1/4 cup sugar		50	
1 1/2 teaspoons baking powder			
1 teaspoon salt			
4 teaspoons xanthum gum			
2 teaspoons vanilla			
1 egg	7		7
1/4 cup dry low-fat milk	9	14	
2 1/4 teaspoons instant yeast			
1 cup warm water			
3/4 cup rice flour	8	90	
1 1/2 cup tapioca flour		49	
1/2 cup soy flour	40	36	22
1/2 cup oat flour	5	27	3
Filling:			
3 tablespoons butter, softened			33
1/2 cup sugar		100	
1 tablespoon cinnamon			
Total for 16 buns	69	366	109
Total per bun	4	23	7

	P	C	F
Glaze (optional):			
2 tablespoons butter melted			22
1 cup chopped pecans (or other nuts)	7	17	70
1/4 cup sugar		50	
1/4 cup brown sugar		35	
Total for 16 buns plus glaze	80	468	201
Total per bun plus glaze	5	29	12

☆ To make the dough, combine the butter, sugar, baking powder, salt, xanthum gum, vanilla, and egg in a bowl.

☆ Add the dry milk, yeast, and water.

☆ Combine with the flours.

☆ Let the dough rise until puffy.

☆ While the dough is rising, mix together the filling ingredients in a separate bowl and set aside.

☆ When the dough is almost double in bulk, place it on a sheet of plastic wrap approximately 18 inches long and cover with a second piece of plastic wrap.

☆ With a rolling pin, roll out the dough until it is approximately 1/8 inch thick and 16 inches long.

☆ Remove the top plastic wrap, and using a stiff spatula spread the filling evenly over the dough.

☆ Carefully roll up the dough into a log, gently peeling away the remaining plastic wrap.

☆ Cut the roll into 16 equal pieces and set aside.

☆ To make the glaze, melt the butter and place it in a 9 x 11-inch oblong pan or a 12-inch square pan.

☆ Sprinkle the chopped nuts evenly over the butter, then mix the sugars together and sprinkle them on top.

☆ Place the buns on the glaze, reshaping them round and letting them rise again for 45 minutes. If you are not using glaze, butter the pan before placing the buns on it.

☆ Preheat the oven to 375 degrees.

☆ Bake for 10 to 15 minutes.

Hint: For fewer carbohydrates, omit the glaze.

STICKY SWEET SWIRLY BUNS WITHOUT GLUTEN

Yield: 24 buns

This is the nonyeast bun option, for individuals who cannot eat yeast or are trying to rid their body of funguses and excess yeast.

	P	C	F
Dough:			
1$\frac{1}{2}$ cups rice flour	6	180	3
$\frac{3}{4}$ cup soy flour	60	54	33
$\frac{3}{4}$ cup tapioca flour		24	
1$\frac{1}{2}$ teaspoons salt			
3$\frac{1}{2}$ teaspoons xanthum gum			
$\frac{1}{4}$ cup sugar		50	
$\frac{2}{3}$ cup dry low-fat milk	24	37	
4 tablespoons baking powder			
2 tablespoons baking soda			
$\frac{1}{4}$ cup butter			44
1$\frac{3}{4}$ cups water			
1 teaspoon vinegar			
4 eggs	28		28
Filling:			
1 stick butter, softened			88
$\frac{1}{2}$ cup brown sugar		70	
2 teaspoons cinnamon			
1 cup chopped walnuts/pecans	20	12	80
Total for 24 buns	138	427	276
Total per bun	6	18	11

☆ Preheat the oven to 375 degrees.

☆ To make the dough, mix the flours, salt, xanthum gum, $\frac{1}{4}$ cup of sugar, dry milk, baking powder, and baking soda using a mixer with a dough hook attached.

☆ Melt the butter in the water on the stovetop or in a microwave.

☆ After the dry ingredients are mixed, pour in the melted butter and water mixture, then add the vinegar.

☆ Stir in the eggs.

☆ In a separate bowl, prepare the filling. Blend the butter, sugar, and cinnamon, setting the nuts aside.

☆ Tear off a piece of waxed paper approximately 20 inches long. Dampen the counter with water, lay the waxed paper on the counter, and spoon half the batter onto the waxed paper.

☆ Grease your fingers well, and pat the dough into a rectangle approximately 16 x 10 inches.

☆ Spread half of the filling mixture on the dough, then sprinkle half of the nuts on top.

☆ Slowly roll up the dough lengthwise into a log and cut it into 12 pieces.

☆ Grease 2 muffin tins and put a dab of butter in each cup.

☆ Fill 1 tin with the dough pieces.

☆ Grease your fingers again and repeat the process with the remaining ingredients, filling the second muffin tin.

☆ Bake for 10 minutes.

Sweet Swirly Buns

Yield: 16 buns

For individuals who do not like sticky sugar, this recipe features the familiar white glaze.

	P	C	F
Dough:			
1 cup rice flour	9	126	2
1¼ cups tapioca flour		41	
1 cup soy flour	80	72	44
3 tablespoons sugar		48	
1¼ teaspoons salt			
2 teaspoons instant yeast			
1½ teaspoons baking powder			
¼ cup dry low-fat milk	9	14	3
3½ teaspoons xanthum gum			
2 teaspoons vanilla			
1½ eggs, beaten	10		10
¾ cup warm water			
3 tablespoons olive oil			42
Filling:			
2 tablespoons butter, softened			22
½ egg, beaten	4		4
½ cup sugar		100	
1 tablespoon cinnamon			
Glaze:			
3 tablespoons cream			15
1 cup glazing sugar		100	
Total filling/glaze	4	200	41
Total dough	108	301	101
Total for 16 buns	112	501	142
Total per bun	7	31	9

☆ To make the dough, first mix together the dry ingredients for 1 to 2 minutes.
☆ Add the vanilla, eggs, water, and oil, and mix for another 1 to 2 minutes.
☆ Set the dough aside and let it rise until puffy. (It will not double in size.)
☆ While the dough is rising, mix the filling ingredients in a bowl and set aside.
☆ After the dough has risen, place it on a sheet of plastic wrap approximately 18 inches long, then cover it with a second piece of plastic wrap.
☆ With a rolling pin, roll out the dough until it is approximately $1/8$ inch thick and 16 inches long, then remove the top piece of plastic wrap.
☆ Using a stiff spatula, spread the filling evenly over the dough.
☆ Carefully roll up the dough into a log, gently peeling away the other piece of plastic wrap.
☆ Cut the dough into 16 pieces and place them in a 9 x 11-inch oblong pan or a 12-inch square pan.
☆ Let the dough rise for another 20 to 30 minutes while preheating the oven to 375 degrees.
☆ Bake the buns for 6 to 8 minutes.
☆ Remove the buns from the oven and let them cool completely.
☆ While the buns are cooling, make the glaze by combining the cream and sugar in a small bowl.
☆ After the buns are cool, drizzle the glaze over them.

MERLIN'S MUFFINS

Yield: 12 muffins

It is believed that Merlin lived outside of time and that his gift of prophecy was the result of living from the future to the present. When eagerly consumed, this melt-in-your-mouth staple will exist briefly in the present and soon disappear into the past.

	P	C	F
½ cup sugar		100	
2 tablespoons coconut oil			84
¼ cup rice flour	2	30	
¼ cup tapioca flour		8	
½ cup soy flour	40	36	22
¼ teaspoon salt			
2 teaspoons baking powder			
2 eggs	14		14
¼ teaspoon vanilla			
¼ teaspoon xanthum gum			
½ cup 2 percent milk	4	6	2
Total for 12 muffins	60	180	122
Total per muffin	5	15	10

☆ Preheat the oven to 350 degrees.
☆ Cream the sugar and coconut oil.
☆ Beat in the flours, salt, baking powder, eggs, vanilla, and xanthum gum.
☆ Add the milk.
☆ Pour the batter into a well-greased muffin tin, filling the cups approximately ½ full.
☆ Bake for 15 to 20 minutes.

Hint: Muffins store best in a plastic container in the refrigerator. For a lemon–poppy seed variation, after adding the xanthum gum mix in 2 teaspoons of lemon juice and 3 teaspoons of poppy seeds.

MIRACLE MANNA

Yield: 2 loaves

This bread, a family favorite, inspires wonder with its relative ease of preparation and range of uses. I bake four loaves at a time, usually in the morning, keeping one or two in the refrigerator for immediate consumption and the rest in the freezer. Excellent for French toast and good for croutons, Miracle Manna is also an acceptable sandwich bread, although it tends to be a little flat on top because it's gluten free.

	P	C	F
2 cups rice flour	22	240	4
1 cup tapioca flour		33	
$^1/_4$ cup sugar		50	
$3^1/_2$ teaspoons xanthum gum			
$^2/_3$ cup dry low-fat milk	24	37	
$1^1/_2$ teaspoons salt			
$1^1/_2$ tablespoons dry active yeast			
$^1/_2$ stick butter			44
$1^1/_4$ cups water			
$^1/_2$ cup water			
1 teaspoon white vinegar			
3 eggs	21		21
Total for 2 loaves (32 slices)	67	360	69
Total per slice	2	11	2

☆ Set up a mixer with the strongest beaters or bread hooks, and on low, mix together the flours, sugar, xanthum gum, dry milk, salt, and yeast.

☆ In a microwave, melt the butter in $1^1/_4$ cups of water approximately 3 minutes.

☆ Add the melted butter mixture to the dry ingredients and mix until blended.

☆ Add $^1/_2$ cup of water and blend.

☆ Mix in the vinegar and the eggs.

(cont.)

☆ Put the dough in a large bowl and set it in a warm place to rise until it doubles. (I warm my oven to the lowest setting, put the dough inside to rise, then turn the oven off.) The dough will be moist and sticky, unlike wheat bread dough.

☆ While the dough is rising, butter 2 9 x 5-inch loaf pans and place them on a cookie sheet or jelly roll pan.

☆ When the dough has doubled, beat it on high for 3 minutes, using a mixer.

☆ Spoon the dough into the buttered pans and let it rise again until it is double in size.

☆ Preheat the oven to 400 degrees.

☆ Bake for about 10 minutes or until the tops are brown, then cover the loaves with tinfoil.

☆ Continue to bake for another 50 minutes, then remove the loaves to a cooling rack.

☆ When they are cool, place them in plastic bags and refrigerate or freeze.

Hint: You can substitute baking yeast for the dry active yeast. To do this, begin by dissolving 2 teaspoons of sugar in $1/2$ cup of warm water, then add $1^{1}/_{2}$ tablespoons of yeast and set the mixture aside to foam. Add it to the dough before the vinegar and eggs, remembering to omit the dry active yeast.

Soups, Dressings and Sauces

PUCKERING PEPPERED SOUP

Yield: 10 servings

Our family makes this hot and sour soup whenever one of us begins to feel under the weather. It seems to be just what the body needs to fight off viruses, and it is perfect for warming the soul on cold winter days.

	P	C	F
2 tablespoons butter			22
1 pound tofu, cubed	64	11	32
1 cup shitake mushrooms (optional)	2	21	
4 cups water			
4 teaspoons or large cubes vegetable bouillon or stock			
3 teaspoons Thai fish sauce			
2 tablespoons tamari (wheat-free)			
3 teaspoons hot sesame oil			10
1 tablespoon toasted sesame oil			14
3 tablespoons balsamic vinegar			
1 egg	7		7
Total for 10 servings	**73**	**32**	**85**
Total per serving	**7**	**3**	**9**

☆ Heat the butter in a soup pot at medium high.

☆ Drop in the tofu cubes and mushrooms, if desired, and sauté.

☆ Add the water, bouillon, fish sauce, tamari, oils, and vinegar. Once hot, adjust the oil and vinegar to the desired taste.

☆ Scramble the egg, and when the soup begins to boil pour the egg in, stirring constantly until it becomes stringy.

Hint: For a heartier soup, replace the water and bouillon with beef stock left over from making Reggae Steak (see page 79) or Heavenly Hash (see page 77).

TOADSTOOL AND CHEESE SOUP

Yield: 12 servings

A dear friend in Michigan introduced me to a soup similar to this. A recipe from a local restaurant, it was, in his words, "heavenly." I attempted many times to duplicate it, and although the taste is not exactly the same, here is a delicious substitute that leads you to fairyland.

	P	C	F
2^1/$_2$ 8-ounce packages mushrooms	12	26	2
^{1}/$_2$ stick butter			44
1^1/$_2$ pints light cream	8	24	138
2 pints heavy cream	20	24	352
1 teaspoon salt			
^{1}/$_2$ teaspoon freshly ground pepper (or to taste)			
^{3}/$_4$ cup grated Parmesan cheese or shaker cheese	66	6	48
Total for 12 servings	106	80	584
Total per servings	9	6	48

☆ Wash and slice the mushrooms.

☆ Melt the butter in a large pot and sauté the mushrooms, covered, until they begin to "bleed," stirring every 5 minutes to keep them from sticking.

☆ Turn the heat to medium and add the creams, salt, and pepper. Heat the soup until it begins to simmer, stirring frequently so it doesn't burn. Then stir in the cheese until it is melted and blended.

Hint: Add extra cheese if desired.

Salad Elixirs

Here are four alternatives to store-bought salad dressings, which usually contain trans-oils. Lemon Garlic Elixir is a good choice for people who are trying to eliminate overgrowths of yeast from their body and have difficulty tolerating fermented foods like vinegar. The others dress up any creation.

Lemon Garlic Elixir

Yield: 1 cup

	P	C	F
8 tablespoons olive oil			112
8 tablespoons water			
$^1/_2$ teaspoon salt			
4 tablespoons lemon or lime juice			
$^1/_4$ teaspoon cayenne pepper			
1 teaspoon maple syrup		4	
1 clove garlic, minced			
Total for 1 cup		4	112
Total per 2 tablespoons			10

Lemon Salsa Elixir

Yield: 1 cup

	P	C	F
$^2/_3$ cup olive or macadamia nut oil			168
$^1/_3$ cup plus $1^1/_2$ tablespoons lemon or lime juice			
1 teaspoon mustard			
1 teaspoon salt			
3 tablespoons hot salsa			
Total for 1 cup			168
Total per 2 tablespoons			11

Mustard Vinaigrette

Yield: 1 cup

	P	C	F
²/₃ cup olive oil			168
¹/₃ cup balsamic vinegar			
¹/₃ cup water			
1 teaspoon salt			
1 tablespoon mustard			
Total for 1 cup			**168**
Total per 2 tablespoons			**11**

Horseradish Mayonnaise Elixir

Yield: 1 cup

	P	C	F
¹/₃ cup Sandwich Salve (see page 51)	2		43
1 tablespoon olive oil			14
1 tablespoon horseradish			
2 tablespoons water			
Total for 1 cup	2		57
Total per 2 tablespoons			5

☆ Place all the ingredients in a jar with a screw-top lid and shake until well mixed.

SANDWICH SALVE

Yield: 1 1/3 cups

After I searched in vain for an organic mayonnaise containing monoun-saturated fats, the desire to feed my family these good fats prompted me to make my own mayonnaise. This one is tidy and simple, yet so good that visitors want to know what brand it is and where to get it.

	P	C	F
1 egg	7		7
1 teaspoon Dijon mustard			
1/2 teaspoon salt			
3 tablespoons apple cider vinegar			
1 cup peanut oil			168
Total for 1 1/3 cups	7		175
Total per tablespoon			11

☆ Place the egg, mustard, salt, vinegar, and 1/2 of the oil in a blender, and process.

☆ When the ingredients have turned pale and thick, slowly drizzle the rest of the oil in the center of the mixture and continue to process until smooth. On some days the mayonnaise will be thick after blending, other times thinner—an inexplicable variability that can perhaps be attributed only to the weather or phase of the moon.

☆ Pour the mayonnaise into a jar and refrigerate. Once cooled, it will be thick and creamy.

Hint: A tripled recipe fills a mayonnaise jar. Also, you can substitute olive oil for the peanut oil, but the mayonnaise will have a strong olive flavor. Other gourmet substitutes are macadamia nut, walnut, and avocado oils.

Fiery Abyss

Yield: 10 cups

A festival of vegetables, this medium to hot salsa can be used to dip carrot or cucumber sticks in for a snack, top off a salad, or as an accent to make any meal bolder and more adventurous.

	P	C	F
3 large red bellpeppers	3	15	3
4 small green bellpeppers	3	15	3
1¹/₂ large sweet onions	3	28	
12 plum tomatoes	12	72	5
¹/₂ bunch cilantro			
1¹/₂ tablespoons salt			
¹/₂ cup olive oil			84
¹/₂ cup balsamic vinegar		16	
4 tablespoons hot sauce			
3 cloves garlic (optional)			
Total for 10 cups	21	146	95
Total per ¹/₄ cup	1	4	2

☆ Cut the peppers, onions, and tomatoes into bite-size pieces and place them in a large bowl.

☆ Mince the cilantro and sprinkle it evenly over the vegetables.

☆ Add the salt, olive oil, vinegar, and hot sauce and blend, adjusting the salt and hot sauce to the desired taste.

PRESTO PESTO

Yield: 2 cups

Research shows that cilantro binds with mercury and other heavy metals, enabling the body to get rid of them. So a good motto might be: Cilantro each day keeps the metals at bay. When my patients requested a garlic-free pesto to avoid alienating family and coworkers, I created this quick but tasty version, eliminating the standard call for garlic and substituting cilantro for the traditional basil.

	P	C	F
1 cup fresh cilantro			
1/2 cup pine nuts	12	7	30
1 cup olive oil			168
3 tablespoons lemon juice		3	
1/4 teaspoon salt			
1 large hot pepper			
1 teaspoon hot sauce			
Total for 2 cups	12	10	198
Total per tablespoon			8

☆ Place the cilantro and pine nuts in a blender and process.
☆ Blend in the remaining ingredients until the mixture attains the consistency of a paste.
☆ Let stand 1 hour before serving or freeze for future use.

Hint: If you are unconcerned about spicy breath, add 1 large garlic clove, minced. With or without the garlic, this pesto is superb on 1/2 cup of cooked rice pasta and 2 ounces of ground beef, or as a salad dressing thinned with a little water or balsamic vinegar.

Red Bog

Yield: 1¹/₄ cups

A walk through a bog when the mists are stirring and the animals are stilled brings an expectation of tantalizing moments to come. This mildly spicy, not too sweet barbecue sauce fulfills that expectation. It is outstanding on chicken or steak, and with a little horseradish added it transforms into a fine cocktail sauce.

	P	C	F
4 tablespoons organic ketchup		12	
1 tablespoon stone-ground mustard		2	
1 tablespoon chili and garlic sauce			
1 tablespoon balsamic vinegar			
1 tablespoon olive oil			14
Total for 1¹/₄ cups		14	14
Total per tablespoon		1	1

☆ Place all the ingredients in a small bowl and blend.

CHOCOLATE SHINE

Yield: ³/₄ cup

This glaze adds a pleasing glow to almost any dessert imaginable, such as Dream Puffs (see page 107), strawberries, or Marvelous Minis (see pages 116 and 117). For Dream Puffs, I recommend dipping the tops into the glaze and cooling them before filling. Or you can slice each puff in half, dip the top in the glaze, fill the bottom with Luminescence (see page 85), and then assemble.

	P	C	F
6 ounces bittersweet chocolate	16	83	27
1 tablespoon honey		17	
1 stick butter			88
Total for ³/₄ cup	**16**	**100**	**115**

- ☆ Partially fill a medium-size saucepan with water and set it on the stovetop over medium-high heat.
- ☆ Put all the ingredients in a small glass bowl.
- ☆ Place the bowl in the saucepan, letting the water come about halfway up the outside of the bowl. Allow the ingredients to melt slowly (heated to no more than 120 degrees), stirring occasionally.
- ☆ When the ingredients have melted, let the mixture cool slightly (to 90 degrees).
- ☆ Use as a glaze for fresh fruit or baked goods. After dipping the items, place them glaze side up on a cookie sheet and let them cool in the refrigerator.

Hint: You can freeze the leftover glaze for later use, reheating it in a glass bowl set in a saucepan that has been partially filled with water, as described above.

ENTRÉES

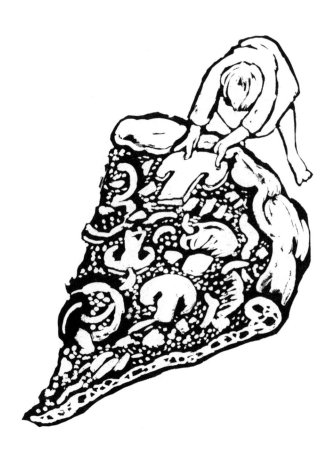

EVERYDAY CLOAKS

Yield: 10 crepes

Delectable, versatile crepes can be served plain, as blintzes, or as rollups with a filling such as eggs or sausage. When I watched my friend improvising these one day with a baby on her hip and a toddler clinging to her leg, I thought, "How quick and healthy. Perfect for one-handed moments—a mother's dream!" The following is a wheatless version of this classic.

	P	C	F
2 large eggs	14		14
1 cup 2 percent milk	8	12	4
2 tablespoons water			
1 cup rice flour	11	120	2
1 cup tapioca flour		33	
3 tablespoons olive oil			42
$1/2$ teaspoon salt			
Total for 10 crepes	**33**	**165**	**62**
Total per crepe	**3**	**16**	**6**

☆ Using a mixer, beat the eggs and milk.

☆ Add the water, flours, oil, and salt and blend until smooth.

☆ Preheat a pan to medium high and melt a liberal amount of butter. Be generous because rice flour tends to stick easily.

☆ Ladle in enough batter to make a thin pancake. When the edges are cooked and the center is still slightly liquid, turn it. If you wait too long, the rice flour may cause it to burn.

☆ Remove, then repeat with the remaining batter, adding fresh butter to the pan each time and stacking the finished crepes.

Hint: To complement the carbohydrates, you can fill each crepe with a preferred protein, such as 1 egg, scrambled; 1 ounce of ham or sausage; $1/4$ cup of cottage cheese; or $1^1/_2$ ounces of tofu. Alternatively, you can sprinkle 2 to 4 tablespoons of protein powder into the batter, although you may need to add a little water to maintain the proper consistency.

DRESS CLOAKS

Yield: 10 crepes

Additional time and ingredients are necessary for these crepes, but like a dinner party with fine china, the added touch of class makes it worth the effort. The yogurt in this recipe provides a smooth texture and extra protein.

	P	C	F
½ cup rice flour	5	60	1
½ cup tapioca flour		16	
⅓ cup soy flour	26	24	15
3 tablespoons protein powder (optional)	32		
⅓ cup low-fat dry milk	12	18	
4 eggs	28		28
1 cup 2 percent milk	8	12	4
½ cup vanilla yogurt	4	14	1
Total for 10 crepes	**115**	**144**	**49**
Total per crepe **with protein powder**	11	14	5
Total per crepe **without protein powder**	8	14	5

☆ Combine all the dry ingredients with a mixer.
☆ Add the eggs and milk, a little at a time.
☆ Add the yogurt.
☆ Melt butter in a pan and ladle in enough batter to cover the bottom.
☆ When the batter begins to bubble slightly and harden around ⅔ of the crepe, flip it and cook the other side briefly.
☆ Repeat with the remaining batter, adding fresh butter to the pan each time and stacking the finished crepes.

FAIRY RING CRUST

Yield: 1 crust (8 slices)

A perfect circle of mushrooms under a dense, moist canopy of ancient trees lets you know the wee people are working their magic—which is also what happens when you watch this liquid batter transformed in the oven to a doughy pizza crust. With endless topping combinations only a thought away, this crust is a must in any wheatless home.

	P	C	F
1/4 cup 2 percent milk	2	3	1
2 large eggs	14		14
2/3 cup tapioca flour		22	
1/3 cup rice flour	3	40	
1/4 cup olive oil			42
1 teaspoon xanthum gum			
Total for 8 slices	**19**	**65**	**57**
Total per slice	**2**	**8**	**7**

☆ Preheat the oven to 400 degrees.
☆ Blend the milk and eggs with a mixer.
☆ Add the remaining ingredients and mix until smooth.
☆ Grease a raised-edge pizza pan with butter and pour in the dough.
☆ Bake for 5 to 7 minutes, then remove from the oven. The crust is done when it lifts easily from the pan with a spatula. If the crust sticks, cook it for a few more minutes. Add desired topping; see Desert Fairy Ring (page 62), Ocean Fairy Ring (page 63), Wilderness Fairy Ring (page 65), and Woodland Fairy Ring (page 66), or create your own.

Hint: For a crust with balanced P/C/F ratios, stir approximately 1 1/2 tablespoons of protein powder into the batter. As for toppings, I like mine with lots of protein, allowing for more carbohydrates with my meal, such as a flourless cookie or a little ice cream.

Desert Fairy Ring

Yield: 8 slices

If you miss the spicy combo of ground beef, cheese, and refried beans wrapped in a chewy flour tortilla, you will delight in the fixin's of this wheatless pizza.

	P	C	F
1 Fairy Ring Crust (see page 61)	19	65	57
¹/₂ cup organic refried pinto or black beans	8	20	
1 cup low-fat mozzarella or Italian mix cheese, shredded	20	1	15
2 ounces organic hamburger, browned	18		9
1 teaspoon salt			
Total for 8 slices	**65**	**86**	**81**
Total per slice	**8**	**11**	**10**

☆ Bake the crust as directed.
☆ With a spatula, spread the beans on top.
☆ Sprinkle the cheese evenly over the beans.
☆ Place the hamburger in a pan, add the salt, and brown. Then spread this topping evenly over the cheese.
☆ Bake at 400 degrees for 15 minutes.

Hint: To reduce the overall fat content, use fat-free cheese. For a balanced meal with dessert, increase the amount of hamburger to 12 ounces, eat 1 slice of pizza, and follow with ¹/₄ cup of low-carbohydrate ice cream (approximately 9 carbohydrates), like Edy's Deering, or Sealtest—but not Ben and Jerry's!

OCEAN FAIRY RING

Yield: 8 slices

In this pizza variation, the ginger adds a succulent but tangy accent to spicy peanut sauce, creating a flavor that surprises and excites.

	P	C	F
1 Fairy Ring Crust (see page 61)	19	65	57
$1/2$ cup water			
$1/3$ cup peanut butter	16	13	32
1 tablespoon brown sugar (optional)		11	
1 teaspoon minced garlic			
$1/2$ teaspoon minced jalapeño pepper			
$1^{1}/_{2}$ teaspoons tamari			
$1/4$ teaspoon lemon juice			
1 tablespoon fresh cilantro, chopped			
1 cup low-fat mozzarella or Italian mix cheese, shredded	56	8	56
$1/2$ red or yellow bellpepper, sliced			
1 scallion, chopped			
2 tablespoons grated fresh ginger			
4 ounces shrimp, cooked and peeled	23		1
Total for 8 slices	114	97	146
Total per slice	14	12	18

☆ Bake the crust as directed.
☆ Boil the water in a small pot on medium heat.
☆ Mix in the peanut butter and sugar, if desired, until smooth. Stir until the mixture thickens, then remove it from the stove.

(cont.)

☆ Add the garlic, jalapeño pepper, tamari, lemon juice, and cilantro, stirring until smooth.
☆ Spread the sauce on the crust.
☆ Sprinkle the cheese over the sauce.
☆ Distribute the peppers, scallions, ginger, and shrimp evenly on top.
☆ Bake at 400 degrees for 15 to 20 minutes.

Hint: If 1 slice of this pizza leaves you wanting more, go for 2. But if you'd like a dessert with this meal, increase the amount of shrimp to 8 ounces, have 1 slice of pizza, and for dessert indulge in $1/4$ cup of low-carbohydrate ice cream.

WILDERNESS FAIRY RING

Yield: 8 slices

This is a gourmet pizza featuring a unique spicy Thai peanut sauce and grilled chicken. For individuals with a discerning palate, chunky peanut butter adds extra texture.

	P	C	F
1 Fairy Ring Crust (see page 61)	19	65	57
1/2 cup water			
1/3 cup peanut butter	16	13	32
1 teaspoon minced garlic			
1/2 teaspoon tamari			
1/4 teaspoon lemon juice			
1 cup low-fat mozzarella or Italian mix cheese, shredded (optional)	56	8	56
3 ounces sautéed or grilled chicken, cut into pieces	18		1
Total per 8 slices	109	86	146
Total per slice	14	11	18

☆ Bake the crust as directed.

☆ Boil the water in a pan on medium heat.

☆ Stir in the peanut butter, garlic, tamari, and lemon juice and continue stirring until the mixture thickens.

☆ Let the mixture cool slightly before spreading it evenly over the crust with a spatula.

☆ Sprinkle the cheese, if desired, over the sauce and distribute the chicken evenly on top.

☆ Bake at 400 degrees for 15 minutes, less if you omit the cheese.

Hint: If you can't eat peanuts, substitute almond butter and use a little less water. To reduce the fat content, omit the cheese and you will still have a splendid pizza.

WOODLAND FAIRY RING

Yield: 8 slices

Organic hot Italian sausage blended with pepperoncini makes this pizza a favorite at birthday parties and other gatherings. Always satisfying, it will warm you on the coldest winter days and energize you on lazy summer afternoons.

	P	C	F
1 Fairy Ring Crust (see page 61)	19	65	57
3 organic hot Italian sausages	42		60
1/2 cup organic tomato sauce	2	9	
1 cup low-fat mozzarella or Italian mix cheese	20	1	15
1/2 red bellpepper		2	
4 mushrooms, sliced			
5 pepperoncinis, sliced			
Total for 8 slices	**83**	**77**	**132**
Total per slice	**10**	**9**	**17**

☆ Bake the crust as directed.
☆ Grill the sausages and cut them into bite-size pieces.
☆ Spread the sauce on the crust.
☆ Sprinkle the cheese evenly over the sauce.
☆ Distribute the bellpepper, mushrooms, pepperoncinis, and grilled sausages over the cheese.
☆ Bake at 400 degrees for 15 to 20 minutes.

DRAGON-ROASTED VEGETABLES

Yield: 6 servings

This dish of carrot swords, broccoli plumes, and fires of garlic makes a rousing presentation for any knight's table. Dragon-roasting transforms the ordinary into extraordinary.

	P	C	F
1 onion	1	14	
1/2 head broccoli	2	4	
1/4 head cauliflower	4	6	
1 red bellpepper	1	5	1
1 green bellpepper	1	5	1
1 head garlic, peeled	4	19	
3 tablespoons lemon juice			
3 tablespoons olive oil			42
1 teaspoon salt			
2 teaspoons rosemary			
1 teaspoon basil			
1/2 teaspoon ground pepper			
Total for 6 servings	13	53	44
Total per serving	2	9	7

☆ Preheat the oven to 425 degrees.
☆ Wash the vegetables and peel the garlic.
☆ Cut the vegetables into bite-size pieces and put them in a roasting pan. Sprinkle in the peeled garlic cloves, whole.
☆ Mix together the lemon juice, olive oil, and spices and pour over the vegetables.
☆ Cover with a lid or tinfoil, and bake until tender, approximately 20 to 40 minutes.

Hint: If you do not have a roasting pan, any pan will do, even a cast-iron frying pan.

Caped Crustaceans

Yield: 6 servings

Skewered shrimp wrapped in prosciutto and horseradish will perform magic at summer parties under the stars. White rice and Fiery Abyss (see page 52) perfectly complement this light but satisfying dish.

	P	C	F
2 cups water			
1 pound raw shrimp, unpeeled	92		4
1 large red bellpepper	1	5	1
1 large green bellpepper	1	5	1
$1/4$ pound prosciutto	28		28
3 tablespoons horseradish			
Total for 6 servings	**122**	**10**	**34**
Total per serving	**20**	**1**	**6**

☆ To prepare the shrimp, bring the water to a boil and then drop them in. The shells will turn slightly red when they are done.

☆ Strain off the water and set the shrimp aside to cool.

☆ Chop the peppers into $1/2$-inch square pieces.

☆ Slice the prosciutto into thin strips, one for each shrimp.

☆ Put the horseradish in a medium-size bowl, peel the shrimp, and coat each one evenly with horseradish.

☆ Wrap each shrimp in a strip of prosciutto and skewer it. If you do not have skewers, chopsticks will do. Then skewer a piece of pepper, alternating the ingredients until they have all been used.

☆ Heat the skewers on a hot grill, turning once, until the shrimp and prosciutto are browned.

Hint: Served as an appetizer to welcome special guests, this dish is sure to be a crowd pleaser.

CHICKEN CHARMS

Yield: 8 servings

When I was a child and KFC was a treat on long car trips, it epitomized finger-licking euphoria. Now that it is forbidden due to its wheat flour, I munch on this satisfying variation that is especially prized by my patients under age eighteen.

	P	C	F
1 pound boneless breast of chicken	104		6
1/4 cup 2 percent milk	2	3	1
1/2 cup coconut oil (or peanut oil)			84
1/2 cup rice flour	5	60	1
1/2 cup tapioca flour		16	
1 tablespoon salt			
1/4 teaspoon pepper			
Total for 8 servings	111	79	92
Total per 2-ounce serving	14	10	12

☆ Remove the fat from the chicken and rinse it under cold water. Then cube it into bite-size pieces and place it in a large glass bowl.

☆ Pour the milk over the cubed chicken and set it aside to soak.

☆ Pour the oil in a frying pan and heat to medium high. The oil will liquefy, coating the bottom of the pan approximately 1/4 to 1/2 inch.

☆ In a separate bowl, mix together the flours, salt, and pepper.

☆ Remove the chicken from the milk and place it in the flour mixture.

☆ Roll the chicken, coating each piece thoroughly. If necessary, add more flour to ensure an even coating.

(cont.)

☆ Test the oil temperature with a sprinkling of flour mixture, which will sizzle when the oil is hot enough. Then gently drop in several pieces of chicken.

☆ Turn them when they are golden brown on the bottom, approximately 3 minutes. When the chicken is browned on both sides, remove it from the pan and drain it on paper towels.

☆ Repeat the process until all the chicken is cooked.

Hint: The actual fat content of this entrée is lower than stated because only some of the oil is consumed.

CHICKEN IN MIDNIGHT SAUCE

Yield: 5 servings

Put on some calypso music and open a bottle of good white wine, then set forth on this combination of chicken, black beans, and garlic. You will be transported to an exotic island in no time at all.

	P	C	F
2 ounces dried shitake mushrooms	1	4	1
1 cup water			
1 cup tomatoes, diced		8	
1½ large red bellpeppers, sliced thinly		10	
1 cup green beans, cubed		8	
3 scallions, chopped			
12 ounces boneless, skinless chicken breast	104		6
3⅓ tablespoons olive oil			46
4 cloves garlic, finely chopped			
6 tablespoons Guiltless Gourmet No-Fat Spicy Black Bean Dip (or any fat-free bean dip)	8	48	
Dash of chili and garlic sauce, or hot sauce			
Total for 5 servings	113	78	53
Total per serving	23	16	11

☆ Cover the mushrooms with approximately ³/₄ cup of warm water and soak until softened. Then drain the mushrooms and slice them into bite-size pieces.

(cont.)

☆ Place the cut mushrooms and vegetables in a frying pan with $\frac{1}{4}$ cup of water and bring to a boil. Then cover the pan, turn down the heat, and steam the mixture until tender.

☆ In a separate pan, sauté the chicken in the olive oil and garlic.

☆ Blend the black bean dip with the chili and garlic sauce, adding water if needed to reach the desired consistency.

☆ When the chicken is fully cooked, pour on the sauce and simmer for approximately 2 minutes.

☆ Mix in the steamed mushrooms and vegetables and serve.

Hint: For a balanced meal, add 7 grams of carbohydrate—perhaps a small piece of chocolate, $\frac{1}{2}$ a small grapefruit, $\frac{1}{2}$ an apple, or extra vegetables.

CHICKEN SERENDIPITY

Yield: 8 servings

This salad and cold spring water are perfect companions for a summer day following a hike in Maine's Acadia National Park, where the mountains meet the sea. Imagine sitting on pink granite rocks and being lulled by the rise and fall of the waves as gulls soar overhead.

	P	C	F
1¹/₂ pounds boneless, skinless chicken breast	156		10
2 tablespoons butter			22
1 large celery stalk			
1 cup walnuts	20	12	80
1 medium-size carrot			
1 tablespoon salt			
1 teaspoon pepper			
Alfalfa sprouts			
Lettuce leaves			
Tomato (optional)			
1¹/₃ cups Sandwich Salve (see page 51)	7		175
Total for 8 servings	183	12	287
Total per serving	23	2	36

☆ Remove the fat from the chicken and cube it into bite-size pieces.
☆ Melt butter in a sauté pan on low, then add the chicken and cover. Cook the chicken, turning it frequently, until it is no longer pink, approximately ¹/₂ hour.

(cont.)

☆ Meanwhile, chop the celery and walnuts and shred the carrots, placing them all in a large bowl.
☆ Stir in the salt and pepper.
☆ When the chicken is cooked, add it to the bowl and toss it with the other ingredients.
☆ Add the mayonnaise and stir until everything is well mixed. Serve the salad, either at room temperature or chilled, on a bed of lettuce and topped with alfalfa sprouts.

Hint: Try this recipe as a sandwich filling with sprouts and Miracle Manna (see page 43).

Abracadabra Citrus Beef

Yield: 7 servings

If you crave the orange-flavored beef served at Chinese restaurants, which is made with the forbidden cornstarch, there's no need for remorse. With a wave of your culinary wand, you can manifest your own version.

	P	C	F
1 pound sirloin	144		50
1/4 cup 2 percent milk	8	12	4
1/2 cup coconut oil			84
1/2 cup tapioca flour		16	
1/2 cup rice flour	5	60	1
1 teaspoon salt			
2 cups broccoli or spinach, steamed			
Sauce:			
1 cup freshly squeezed orange juice	1	25	
1/2 cup tamari or soy sauce (wheat-free)		12	12
1 tablespoon vinegar			
1 teaspoon fish sauce (optional)			
1 tablespoon maple syrup		4	
2 tablespoons tapioca flour		8	
Total for 7 servings	158	137	151
Total per serving	23	11	21

☆ Remove the fat from the meat, cube it into bite-size pieces, and place it in a glass bowl.

☆ Pour the milk over the meat and set it aside to soak.

☆ Put the oil in a frying pan and heat to medium high. After the oil has melted, it should coat the bottom of the pan approximately 1/4 to 1/2 inch.

☆ Combine the flours and salt in a large bowl.

☆ Remove the meat from the milk and set it in the flour mixture.

(cont.)

☆ Roll the meat, coating each piece thoroughly.

☆ Test the oil temperature with a sprinkling of flour mixture, which will sizzle when the oil is hot enough. Then cook the meat in it, several pieces at a time.

☆ When the meat is browned on both sides, remove it from the pan and place it on paper towels to drain. Repeat the process until all the meat is cooked.

☆ To make the sauce, mix the liquid ingredients in a pan and heat to medium.

☆ Remove approximately $1/4$ cup of the warmed sauce, dissolve the flour in it, then return the mixture to the pan and stir.

☆ When the sauce thickens, reduce the heat.

☆ Place a serving of the steamed broccoli or spinach in a bowl, a serving of browned meat on top, and drench with sauce.

Hint: The actual fat content of this dish is lower than stated because only some of the oil is consumed.

HEAVENLY HASH

Yield: 23 servings

This easy-to-make breakfast treat keeps well in the refrigerator and, reheated, furnishes a quick protein source for people with little time to cook in the mornings. Savor it with a poached egg and two slices of Miracle Manna (see page 43) and you will enter the Promised Land.

	P	C	F
2 large carrots		10	
1 medium-size onion	1	14	
7 mushrooms, sliced	3	6	
1 face rump roast (3–4 pounds)	576		288
Water			
1 tablespoon salt			
2 teaspoons pepper			
Total for 23 servings	580	30	288
Total per serving	25	1	13

☆ Peel and cut the carrots and onion into bite-size pieces, then place them and the mushrooms in a large pot.

☆ Add the roast and enough water to cover everything. Cover the pot with a lid, bring the water to a boil, then reduce the heat, allowing the roast to cook slowly for approximately 4 hours or until the meat falls apart easily.

(cont.)

☆ Transfer the roast and the vegetables to a large frying pan and then tease apart the meat with a fork. Pour $1/4$ cup of the broth over the meat, transferring the remainder to a container to freeze for later use—perhaps as a substitute for the bouillon in Puckering Peppered Soup (see page 47).

☆ While browning the hash on low heat, add the salt and pepper, stirring occasionally.

☆ When crisp, remove and store in a covered container in the refrigerator.

Hint: Children enjoy this hash just as much, if not more, without the vegetables.

REGGAE STEAK

Yield: 12 servings

After eating marvelous jerk steak at a Caribbean restaurant, I asked for the chef's recipe. Told to come back in an hour, when he would be there, I returned periodically throughout the day, finally finding him and also learning the meaning of "Caribbean time." The chef informed me that he didn't use a recipe, but following his verbal instructions, which were devoid of measurements, I managed to re-create the taste, as well as trigger memories of an intoxicating island visit.

	P	C	F
2 tablespoons olive oil			28
1 flank steak (1½ pounds)	216		100
Water			
11½ ounces Newman's Own Steak Sauce		76	9
1 tablespoon jerk seasoning			
Total for 12 servings	216	76	137
Total per serving	18	6	11

☆ Heat the olive oil in a frying pan.

☆ Brown the flank steak slightly on both sides.

☆ Cover the meat with water.

☆ Bring the water to a boil and simmer on low heat, checking every 20 minutes and if necessary adding more water to keep the meat covered. Test the meat periodically with a fork. When it can be shredded easily, it is done.

☆ After shredding the meat, pour the beef stock into a container and freeze for later use—perhaps substituting it for the bouillon in Puckering Peppered Soup (see page 47).

☆ Pour the steak sauce on the meat and blend over low heat.

☆ Stir in the jerk seasoning. The meat will get spicier as it cooks; add more seasoning if desired.

☆ Turn off the heat and let the meat steep in the juices for a while before serving.

STEAK TUMBLE

Yield: 8 servings

Easy to prepare and transport, this substantial salad makes a memorable potluck entrée. Marinated in sweet vinegar, the thin strips of steak melt in the mouth, while the crisp, colorful vegetables promise an explosion of flavor and texture.

	P	C	F
1 pound sirloin	144		50
2 teaspoons salt			
1–2 teaspoons freshly ground pepper			
1/4 cup olive oil			42
1/4 cup sesame oil			54
1/2 cup balsamic vinegar		16	
1 medium-size yellow bellpepper	1	5	1
1 medium-size red bellpepper	1	5	1
1 medium-size orange bellpepper	1	5	1
1 large red onion			
1/4 bunch cilantro			
1 large garlic clove (optional)			
1 tablespoon butter			11
Total for 8 servings	147	31	160
Total per serving	18	4	20

☆ Rub the salt and pepper evenly into the steak.
☆ Slice the meat into 1-inch strips and place it in a large bowl.
☆ Combine the olive oil, sesame oil, and vinegar in another bowl, pour the mixture over the meat, and toss until it is coated.

☆ Cover the bowl with plastic wrap and refrigerate overnight.

☆ The next day thinly slice the peppers and onion and set aside.

☆ Mince the cilantro and the garlic and set aside.

☆ Heat a frying pan to medium high, melt the butter, and sear both sides of the marinated steak strips, several at a time. When they are done, place them in a large bowl. Repeat the process until all the meat is cooked.

☆ After the meat has cooled, pour the marinade over it, then add the vegetables, cilantro, and garlic. Toss all the ingredients together and serve.

Hint: Individuals trying to rid the body of yeast and funguses may substitute lemon or lime juice for the vinegar. The actual fat content of this entrée is approximately 10 to 12 grams per serving because only some of the marinade is consumed.

DESSERTS

LUMINESCENCE

Yield: 5 servings

A cross between vanilla custard and pudding, this radiant and light sweet cream is used to fill the ethereal Dream Puffs (see page 107) but can also be eaten alone as a wonderful tapioca pudding.

	P	C	F
1½ cups heavy cream	7	9	132
3 teaspoons vanilla			
½ cup sugar		100	
¼ cup tapioca flour		8	
4 egg yolks, well beaten			28
Total for 5 servings	7	117	160
Total per serving	1	23	32

☆ Either heat the cream on the stovetop or place it in a microwave-proof bowl and microwave it on high for approximately 1½ to 2 minutes at 50-second intervals, stirring between each so it doesn't burn.

☆ Remove the hot cream and add the vanilla.

☆ Cream together the sugar, tapioca flour, and egg yolks until light in color.

☆ Stir into the hot cream over medium-low heat until the mixture is nearly boiling. Continue stirring until the mixture has thickened, then remove it from the stovetop.

☆ To serve Luminescence as a pudding, spoon it into individual serving dishes and chill until firm. To use Luminescence for filling Dream Puffs, chill it in a bowl and follow the directions on page 107.

Hint: To make chocolate custard, drop 3 ounces of bittersweet chocolate chips into the hot cream while adding the vanilla. To decrease the fat content of Luminescence, substitute ½ cup of half and half or ½ cup of light cream for ½ cup of the heavy cream.

METAMORPHOSIS

Yield: 5 servings

It is spellbinding to watch the transformation of liquid ingredients into thick, creamy pudding. And with Metamorphosis, the magic continues. Before you know it this all-time favorite will do a vanishing act from the refrigerator.

	P	C	F
6 ounces bittersweet chocolate	12	40	54
2 tablespoons cocoa	2	6	
2 tablespoons tapioca flour		4	
1/3 cup sugar		67	
1/8 teaspoon salt			
1 cup light cream	6	8	46
3 large egg yolks			21
2 cup whole milk	16	24	36
1 tablespoon butter, softened			11
2 teaspoons vanilla			
Total for 5 servings	36	149	168
Total per serving	7	29	34

☆ Melt the chocolate by placing it in a glass bowl and microwaving it for 2 minutes on medium power, then stir. If it is not completely melted, repeat for 1 minute. To prevent free radical formation from microwaving, melt the chocolate in a double boiler on the stovetop. If you don't have a double boiler, fill a large pot with water and float a smaller pot on top, melting the chocolate in the smaller pot.

☆ Place the cocoa, tapioca flour, sugar, and salt in a separate pot over low to medium heat.

☆ Stir in the cream slowly and then the yolks and milk. Finally, stir in the chocolate. Bring the mixture to a boil, stirring constantly until it thickens.

☆ Remove it from the heat and stir in the butter and vanilla.

☆ Pour the pudding into 5 small bowls, glasses, or ramekins. Cool a little, then refrigerate.

Hint: To avoid a thick skin forming on top of the pudding, cover with plastic wrap. To make white chocolate pudding, substitute white chocolate for the bittersweet chocolate.

RAVEN'S RAPTURE

Yield: 10 servings

The rich yet cloudlike consistency of this mousse has people melting each spoonful in their mouths, hesitant to interrupt their rapture by swallowing. Guests will beg you for the recipe, which is one of the easiest in this book. Raven's Rapture is also divine as a topping for Wicked Dark Delight (see page 121), as a garnish for Hidden Treasure (see page 114), and on Flying Carpet Roll (see page 112).

	P	C	F
1 cup bittersweet chocolate chips	8	110	36
¼ cup water or decaf coffee, brewed			
2 cups whipping cream	10	12	176
Total for 10 servings	18	122	212
Total per serving	2	12	21

☆ Chill a bowl and beaters in the freezer for whipping the cream.

☆ Put the chocolate chips and the water or decaf coffee in a glass bowl and microwave it for 5 minutes on medium power, then stir. Repeat this process until the chocolate is melted and well mixed with the water or decaf. Alternatively, melt the mixture in a double boiler on the stovetop—or fill a large pot with water and float a smaller pot on top, melting the chocolate and liquid in it. Stir continuously until smooth.

☆ Allow the chocolate mixture to cool but not harden as you whip the cream.

☆ Fold the chocolate mixture into the whipped cream until incorporated. Don't worry if the whipped cream melts a little since it will stiffen when cooled.

☆ Spoon the mousse into small serving dishes, 6-ounce juice glasses, or a large serving bowl and refrigerate for at least 2 hours.

Hint: You can substitute white chocolate for bittersweet chocolate and add 1 tablespoon of your favorite liqueur.

WIZARD COOKIES

Yield: 2 dozen cookies

Chocolate chip cookies enrapture most people, and this particular recipe is so quick and easy, it will dazzle you despite all attempts to fight the spell. These moist, cakey cookies travel well in a lunch box.

	P	C	F
1 cup butter			176
1 cup brown sugar		141	
2 eggs	14		14
1 teaspoon vanilla			
1 teaspoon baking soda			
1/2 teaspoon xanthum gum			
1/2 teaspoon salt			
1 cup tapioca flour		33	
1 cup soy flour	80	72	44
1/4 cup rice flour	2	32	
1 1/2 cups bittersweet chocolate chips	12	165	54
Total for 2 dozen cookies	108	443	228
Total per cookie	5	18	12

☆ Preheat the oven or toaster oven to 375 degrees.
☆ Cream the butter and sugar.
☆ Add the eggs and mix.
☆ Then add the vanilla, baking soda, xanthum gum, and salt and blend.
☆ Add the flours and mix until smooth.
☆ Fold in the chocolate chips.
☆ Scoop out single servings and bake on a greased tray in the toaster oven for 7 minutes. For multiple servings, use a 2-inch diameter ice cream scoop to drop the batter onto a greased cookie sheet, then with the back of the scoop or your fingers, press each ball flat and bake them in the oven for 7 minutes.

NUTTY WIZARD COOKIES WITH GLUTEN

Yield: 3 dozen cookies

These moist, chewy chocolate chip cookies are bewitching. They convince you that you are eating wheat cookies, binding your willpower and tempting your desire. It's rumored the original recipe was purchased from Neiman Marcus and then forwarded to thousands of people on the Web. I reduced the sugar and chocolate as much as possible without sacrificing chewiness and substituted other flours for wheat.

	P	C	F
2 sticks butter			88
1 cup unbleached sugar		200	
1 cup brown sugar		141	
2 eggs	14		14
1 teaspoon baking soda			
1 teaspoon baking powder			
1/2 teaspoon salt			
1 teaspoon xanthum gum			
1 teaspoon vanilla			
2/3 cup tapioca flour		22	
2/3 cup rice flour	7	80	
2/3 cup soy flour	52	48	24
1 1/2 cups oat flour (or oatmeal ground in a blender)	16	81	9
1 1/2 ounces dark chocolate bar		23	9
3/4 cup bittersweet chocolate chips	6	82	27
1/2 cup chopped walnuts	10	6	40
Total for 3 dozen cookies	**105**	**683**	**211**
Total per cookie	**3**	**19**	**6**

☆ Preheat the oven to 375 degrees.

☆ Using a mixer, cream the butter and both sugars.

- ☆ Incorporate the eggs, baking soda, baking powder, salt, xanthum gum, and vanilla.
- ☆ Mix in the flours one by one.
- ☆ Grate the chocolate coarsely, directly into the batter, and incorporate. (I use a Zyliss cheese grater and the drum with the large holes since a regular grater is very time consuming.)
- ☆ Mix in the chocolate chips and walnuts by hand.
- ☆ With a 2-inch diameter ice cream scoop, drop the batter onto a cookie sheet, and using the back of the scoop or your fingers, press each ball flat.
- ☆ Bake for 6 to 8 minutes, then remove the cookies to a cooling rack.

Hint: If you are allergic to nuts, omit them and adjust the baking time to 8 to 10 minutes. This recipe is just as good without them.

WIZARD COOKIES
WITH BETTER BUTTER

Yield: 3 dozen cookies

The jury is still out on whether these taste better with organic almond butter or peanut butter—both are good. However, because some sources say peanut butter carries funguses that can cause food sensitivities, almond is the better butter.

	P	C	F
4 eggs	28		28
1½ cups sucanat		300	
2 16-ounce jars organic almond butter	192	112	432
¾ cup bittersweet chocolate chips	6	82	27
Total for 3 dozen cookies	226	494	487
Total per cookie	6	14	14
Total per cookie without chips	6	11	13

☆ Preheat the oven to 350 degrees.

☆ Mix the eggs and sucanat together. It is important to mix the ingredients in the order given or the oil separates and the cookies come out dry.

☆ Add the almond butter.

☆ Mix in the chocolate chips.

☆ With a 2-inch diameter ice cream scoop, drop the batter onto a cookie sheet, and using the back of the scoop or your fingers, press each ball flat.

☆ Bake for 7 to 10 minutes.

Hint: The peanut butter variation will make the dough a little drier. You can also substitute organic unrefined granulated sugar for sucanat, or omit the chips for a chocolate-free dessert.

WIZARD COOKIES WITH GLUTEN

Yield: 3 dozen cookies

While making Nutty Wizard Cookies with Gluten, I discovered these cakey, moist cookies by accidentally adding extra eggs and intentionally omitting the walnuts because my daughter had asked for cookies without nuts. These cookies are now among her favorites.

	P	C	F
2 sticks butter			176
1 cup brown sugar		141	
1 cup unbleached sugar		200	
4 eggs	28		28
1 teaspoon baking powder			
1 teaspoon baking soda			
$1/_2$ teaspoon salt			
1 teaspoon xanthum gum			
1 teaspoon vanilla			
$2/_3$ cup tapioca flour		22	
$2/_3$ cup rice flour	6	80	2
$2/_3$ cup soy flour	52	48	24
$1^1/_2$ cups oat flour	16	81	9
1 cup bittersweet chocolate chips	8	110	36
Total for 3 dozen cookies	**110**	**682**	**275**
Total per cookie	**3**	**19**	**8**

☆ Preheat the oven to 375 degrees.
☆ Using a mixer, cream the butter and sugars.

(cont.)

☆ Add the eggs and mix. Then add the baking powder, baking soda, salt, xanthum gum, and vanilla.
☆ Mix in the flours one by one.
☆ Mix in the chocolate chips by hand.
☆ With a 2-inch diameter ice cream scoop, drop the batter onto a cookie sheet, and using the back of the scoop or your fingers, press each ball flat.
☆ Bake for 8 to 11 minutes.

Note: When the humidity is high, it takes longer for the cookies to bake.

Wizard Wand Cookies

Yield: 2 dozen cookies

The charm of these chocolate chip cookies is that you can slice off batter from a roll and have a hot cookie whenever you want. Also, children love to slice and bake these by themselves. My sister makes them in batches, freezes them in a plastic container, and pulls them out as needed—a perfect sleight-of-hand option for people who don't have a lot of time to bake.

	P	C	F
¹⁄₂ cup butter			88
¹⁄₂ cup brown sugar		70	
¹⁄₂ cup sugar		100	
1 egg	7		7
1 teaspoon xanthum gum			
¹⁄₂ teaspoon salt			
1 teaspoon vanilla			
³⁄₄ cup rice flour	8	90	
³⁄₄ cup soy flour	60	54	33
³⁄₄ cup bittersweet chocolate chips	6	82	27
Total for 2 dozen cookies	**81**	**396**	**155**
Total per cookie	**3**	**16**	**6**

☆ Cream the butter and sugars.
☆ Add the egg, xanthum gum, salt, and vanilla and blend.
☆ Next, add the flours and blend again.
☆ Fold in the chocolate chips.

(cont.)

☆ Spoon the dough onto plastic wrap approximately 18 inches long.

☆ Mold into a roll with a diameter of $2^1/_2$ inches, cover with plastic wrap, and store in the refrigerator.

☆ Cut the cookie dough into $^3/_4$-inch slices and bake in a preheated oven or toaster oven at 375 degrees for approximately 5 to 7 minutes.

Hint: Instead of molding the dough and storing it in plastic wrap, you can refrigerate it in a plastic container and spoon it out as needed. Or drop the dough onto a greased cookie sheet and make all the cookies at once, freezing the leftovers for later use. My family thinks they taste better baked just before you intend to eat them.

DAYBREAK BARS

Yield: 1 dozen brownies

These treats, accented by rich chocolate, evoke warm feelings of golden sunlight streaming through a window on a winter morning. For individuals who love brownies but don't want the caffeine in solid chocolate keeping them up at night, this blonde variety is a sumptuous compromise.

	P	C	F
½ stick butter			44
½ cup brown sugar		70	
½ cup sugar		100	
2 teaspoons baking powder			
½ teaspoon salt			
3 eggs	21		21
2 teaspoons vanilla			
1 teaspoon xanthum gum			
½ cup tapioca flour		16	
½ cup rice flour	5	60	1
½ cup soy flour	40	36	22
½ cup bittersweet chocolate chips	4	55	18
Total for 1 dozen brownies	70	337	106
Total per brownie	6	28	9

☆ Preheat the oven to 350 degrees.
☆ Cream the butter and sugars.
☆ Add the baking powder and salt.
☆ Stir in the eggs, vanilla, and xanthum gum.
☆ Mix in the flours and chocolate chips.
☆ Pour the dough into a 9 x 9 or 9 x 13-inch buttered baking pan and bake for 10 to 15 minutes.

Hint: The brownies should be slightly underdone when removed from the oven. For a chocolate-free dessert, omit the chocolate chips or substitute with ½ cup of your favorite nuts, chopped.

FORBIDDEN MYSTERIES

Yield: 1 dozen brownies

Some things in life inexplicably stir the soul. We store such mysteries away in a secret place, cherishing them and hoping to relish them again one day. So choose a good hiding place for these chocolate walnut squares—unless you want others to share the soul-stirring experience of devouring them.

	P	C	F
$3/_4$ cup bittersweet chocolate chips	6	82	27
$1^1/_2$ sticks butter			132
4 eggs, separated	28		28
$3/_4$ cup sugar		150	
$3/_4$ cup ground walnuts	15	9	80
$1^1/_2$ tablespoons rice flour	2	15	
$1^1/_2$ tablespoons tapioca flour		4	
$1/_4$ teaspoon cream of tartar			
Total for 1 dozen brownies	**51**	**260**	**267**
Total per brownie	**4**	**22**	**22**

☆ Preheat the oven to 375 degrees.

☆ Melt the chocolate and butter by microwaving it for 2 minutes on medium power or using a double boiler (or fill a large pot with water and then float a smaller pot on top, melting the chocolate and butter in the smaller pot). Stir until smooth.

☆ Beat the egg yolks and $1/_2$ cup of the sugar until the mixture is pale, and incorporate into the warm chocolate mixture.

☆ Stir in the walnuts and the flours and set aside.

☆ Beat the egg whites and cream of tartar until thick, gradually adding the remaining $1/_4$ cup of sugar.

☆ Fold the egg whites into the chocolate, nut, and flour mixture.

☆ Grease an 8-inch square pan or 9 x 7-inch oblong pan, pour in the batter, and bake for 20 to 25 minutes, or until a cake tester comes out slightly moist.

☆ Cool and cut into squares.

Full Moon Bars

Yield: 1¹/₂ dozen brownies

Like a full moon shining on a pristine landscape, dark chocolate brownies are adored by children and adults alike. My cousin graciously shared this Passover confection with me, a perfect ending to any holiday meal.

	P	C	F
1¹/₂ sticks butter			132
³/₄ cup sugar		150	
5 eggs, separated	35		35
6 ounces bittersweet chocolate	12	84	72
³/₄ cup finely ground almonds	36	30	90
Pinch of salt			
Total for 1¹/₂ dozen brownies	**83**	**264**	**329**
Total per brownie	**5**	**15**	**18**

☆ Preheat the oven to 350 degrees.

☆ Cream the butter and sugar.

☆ Melt the chocolate by microwaving it for 2 minutes on medium power or using a double boiler (or fill a large pot with water and then float a smaller pot on top, melting the chocolate and butter in the smaller pot). Stir until smooth and then cool.

☆ Incorporate the cooled chocolate into the butter and sugar mixture and blend. Mix in the egg yolks.

☆ In a Cuisinart, using the metal blade, grind the almonds until there are no large pieces, add them to the batter, and blend. Alternatively, chop the nuts very finely.

☆ In a clean, dry bowl, whip the egg whites until they are stiff but not dry, then fold them into the batter.

☆ Pour the batter into a 9-inch square pan and bake for 45 minutes.

TWILIGHT BARS

Yield: 1¹/₂ dozen brownies

Creamy texture against dense chocolate summons the trajectory power of these cream cheese brownies. One taste is like springing into the moment between day and night when the veil between worlds suddenly thins and dreams become a reality.

	P	C	F
8 ounces cream cheese	16		80
6 ounces bittersweet chocolate	12	60	54
1¹/₂ sticks butter			132
¹/₂ cup plus 1 teaspoon sugar		110	
2¹/₂ teaspoons vanilla			
3 large eggs	21		21
¹/₃ cup soy flour	26	24	14
¹/₃ cup rice flour	3	40	
¹/₄ teaspoon salt			
1 egg yolk			7
Total for 1¹/₂ dozen brownies	**78**	**234**	**308**
Total per brownie	**4**	**13**	**17**

☆ Preheat the oven to 325 degrees.
☆ Warm the cream cheese to room temperature.
☆ Melt the chocolate and butter by microwaving it for 5 minutes on medium power or using a double boiler (or fill a large pot with water and then float a smaller pot on top, melting the chocolate and butter in the smaller pot). Stir occasionally until smooth.
☆ Add ¹/₂ cup of the sugar and 2 teaspoons of the vanilla and mix well.
☆ Stir in the eggs, one at a time.
☆ Combine the dry ingredients in a separate bowl, then add them to the liquid mixture.
☆ In another bowl, mix the cream cheese with the egg yolk, the remaining teaspoon of sugar, and the remaining ¹/₂ teaspoon of vanilla.

☆ Butter a 9 x 7-inch pan and pour in the dough. Spread the cream cheese mixture over the top with a spatula. The two layers will blend a bit.

☆ Bake for 30 to 40 minutes.

Hint: If baked too long, the brownies will be dry.

APPLE STUMBLE

Yield: 12 servings

One summer my dad arrived in his school bus–yellow Suburban with bushels of apples he had picked up in Virginia. The following is a recipe I was pushed into creating to use the apples before they rotted. In this dessert, softened fruit, aromatic spices, and nutty crisp are combined harmoniously in celebration of an otherwise autumn classic.

	P	C	F
Fruit:			
6–8 medium-size apples	1	98	
$1\frac{1}{2}$ tablespoons granulated sugar		18	
$1\frac{1}{2}$ tablespoons lemon juice			
Topping:			
$\frac{1}{4}$ cup tapioca flour		8	
$\frac{1}{4}$ cup soy flour	20	18	11
$\frac{1}{2}$ cup rice flour	5	60	1
$1\frac{1}{2}$ tablespoons sugar		18	
$1\frac{1}{2}$ tablespoons light brown sugar		18	
$\frac{1}{4}$ teaspoon cinnamon			
$\frac{1}{4}$ teaspoon nutmeg			
$\frac{1}{4}$ teaspoon salt			
5 tablespoons butter, chilled			55
$\frac{3}{4}$ cup finely chopped pecans, almonds, or walnuts	15	9	60
Total for 12 servings	41	247	127
Total per serving	3	21	11

☆ Preheat the oven to 375 degrees.

☆ To prepare the fruit, peel, core, and slice the apples, then place them in a large bowl.

☆ Add the sugar and lemon juice, then toss.

☆ Spread the mixture evenly in a 9 x 13-inch greased baking pan.

☆ To make the topping, mix the flours, sugars, cinnamon, nutmeg, and salt in a bowl.

☆ Slice the butter into $1/2$-inch pieces onto the flour mixture.

☆ Coat the slices of butter with the flour mixture and pinch them between your fingers until they have a crumbly consistency. To avoid clumps of dough, refrigerate the mixture for 5 to 10 minutes before pinching it. If while pinching, your hands are warm and the butter begins to soften, refrigerate the mixture again to keep the butter cool.

☆ Mix in the nuts until they are well distributed.

☆ Spread the topping evenly over the apples in the pan.

☆ Bake at 375 degrees for approximately 40 minutes, cover the crisp with tinfoil to prevent burning, and bake for 9 minutes longer at 400 degrees until the fruit bubbles.

TRANSFORMATION PIE
WITH GLUTEN

Yield: 16 slices

This pie is so transformational that a dear friend who hates apples became an aficionado the moment he smelled the tart fruit swimming in thick cinnamony juices offset by its sweet crust. Although very high in carbohydrates, it is wildly popular. One warm slice with a dollop of whipped cream or ice cream and people will clamor for seconds.

	P	C	F
Crust:			
4 tablespoons water			
1 stick butter			88
³/₄ cup oat flour	7	40	4
¹/₂ cup tapioca flour		16	
¹/₂ cup rice flour	5	60	1
¹/₂ teaspoon salt			
	12	116	93
Filling:			
6–8 organic Granny Smith apples	14	112	7
1¹/₂ tablespoons granulated sugar		18	
1¹/₂ tablespoons brown sugar		18	
1 tablespoon cinnamon			
¹/₈ teaspoon salt			
1 tablespoon butter			11
¹/₂ cup cream			30
	14	148	48
Topping:			
¹/₃ cup oat flour	3	18	2
¹/₃ cup tapioca flour		11	

	P	C	F
1/3 cup rice flour	3	40	
1/4 cup granulated sugar		50	
1/4 cup brown sugar		35	
6 tablespoons butter			66
	6	154	68
Total for 16 slices	32	418	209
Total per slice	2	26	13

☆ Put the water in a glass with an ice cube and set aside.

☆ Slice the butter into 1/2-inch pieces, then set them in a small glass bowl in the freezer.

☆ Preheat the oven to 400 degrees.

☆ To prepare the crust, place the flours and salt in a food processor fitted with a metal blade and pulse until mixed. Then add the chilled butter and pulse 3 or 4 times until it is in pea-size pieces and evenly distributed. Alternatively, combine the flours and salt in a medium-size bowl, then incorporate the butter evenly into the flours by squishing the mixture between your fingers until it is in pea-size pieces. If the heat of your hand begins to soften the butter too much and the dough turns wet and sticky, refrigerate the mixture until it is firm and then continue processing.

☆ Transfer the mixture to a bowl and add the ice water, 1 tablespoon at a time, forming a dough ball. Avoid getting the dough too wet; it should hold together but not stick to your hands.

☆ Flatten the dough ball into a circle and put it in the refrigerator to cool.

☆ While the dough is cooling, make the topping by first mixing together all the topping flours and sugars with a wooden spoon or small spatula.

☆ Melt the butter on the stovetop or in a microwave. Then pour the butter into the flour and sugar mixture and blend. The consistency should be moist but crumbly; if it is too wet, add more flour.

☆ Line a jelly-roll pan with parchment paper. In lieu of parchment paper, you can butter the pan lightly.

☆ Spread the topping mixture evenly on the parchment paper, breaking apart any big clumps.

(cont.)

☆ Bake for approximately 5 minutes.

☆ Remove the dough ball from the refrigerator.

☆ Moisten the countertop with a little water and cover with a piece of plastic wrap approximately 18 inches long.

☆ Place the dough on top and cover with a second piece of plastic wrap.

☆ With a rolling pin, roll the dough to the size of your pie tin.

☆ Butter the pie tin.

☆ Remove the top piece of plastic wrap and invert the pie tin over the dough. Then sliding one hand beneath the remaining plastic wrap and placing the other on the pie tin, reverse the crust into the pan and remove the plastic wrap.

☆ Gently shape the dough against the pan and fold the edges down, forming a lip.

☆ Bake for 7 to 10 minutes or until the crust turns slightly brown.

☆ To prepare the filling, peel, core, and cut the apples into $1/4$ x $1/2$-inch pieces.

☆ Place them in a bowl and mix in the sugars, cinnamon, and salt.

☆ Melt the butter in a large pan, then press in the apple mixture to coat it with butter.

☆ Simmer the apples until they are soft but not mushy.

☆ Pour the cream over the apples and incorporate thoroughly.

☆ Press the apple-cream mixture into the baked crust and crumble the topping over it.

☆ Bake for 7 minutes or until the topping begins to brown.

Hint: The pie may be served hot with a dollop of whipped cream or ice cream, or cooled. Our family likes it best after it's spent a day in the refrigerator.

DREAM PUFFS

Yield: 12 puffs

This wheatless delight will remind you of the first time you bit into a cream puff and felt the cool custard coat your mouth as your lips brushed against the sweet crust topped with chocolate—the stuff fantasies are made of. I typically prepare Luminescence first (see page 85), let it cool in the refrigerator, and then make Dream Puffs and a glaze of Chocolate Shine (see page 55).

	P	C	F
1 cup water			
1 stick butter			88
1 tablespoon sugar		8	
1/2 teaspoon salt			
2/3 cup tapioca flour		22	
1/8 cup rice flour	1	15	
4 eggs, room temperature	28		28
Total for 12 puffs	29	45	116
Total per puff	2	4	10
Total per custard filling		10	13
Total per glaze	1	8	10
Total per filled puff with glaze	3	22	33

☆ Preheat the oven to 450 degrees.

☆ Place the water and butter in a saucepan and bring to a boil. Alternatively, microwave it in a glass bowl on high power for 3 to 5 minutes.

☆ Mix the sugar, salt, and flours in a bowl.

☆ Add this mixture to the boiling water and butter. Then stir until the dough thickens and falls away from the sides of the pot. If microwaving, you may need to add the mixture and then heat for another 1 to 2 minutes at 50-second intervals, stirring between each one, until the dough reaches the desired consistency.

(cont.)

☆ Using a hand mixer, beat the eggs, one at a time, into the dough.

☆ Butter a muffin tin and spoon in the dough, filling each cup about $2/3$ full.

☆ Bake for 15 minutes. Then cover the puffs with tinfoil, reduce the heat to 350 degrees, and bake for another 15 minutes.

☆ Remove the puffs, cool, and fill them with Luminescence, whipping cream, or any other desired filling.

Hint: If you intend to glaze the puffs, do so before filling them.

Whoopee Pies

Yield: 10 pies

This popular New England tradition consists of two layers of a light chocolate cake with marshmallow cream sandwiched between them. Whereas the filling usually contains cornstarch or syrup, I've substituted a Chantilly cream, resulting in a winning confection even among wheat and corn eaters.

	P	C	F
Cake:			
2 sticks butter			176
1 1/2 cups brown sugar		210	
2 eggs	14		14
1/4 cup plus 2 tablespoons cocoa	5	11	
1 cup tapioca flour		33	
3/4 cup rice flour	9	40	
1/4 cup soy flour	20	18	11
1 teaspoon baking soda			
1 teaspoon baking powder			
1 teaspoon salt			
1 teaspoon xanthum gum			
1 cup 2 percent milk	8	12	4
1 teaspoon vanilla			
Filling:			
1 cup whipping cream or heavy cream	5	6	88
1 1/2 teaspoons vanilla			
1 1/2 tablespoons glazing sugar		8	
Total for 10 pies	61	338	293
Total per pie	6	34	29
Total for 1/4 pie	1	8	7

(cont.)

☆ Preheat the oven to 350 degrees.

☆ To prepare the cakes, cream the butter, sugar, and eggs with a mixer.

☆ Combine the cocoa, flours, baking soda, baking powder, salt, and xanthum gum in a medium-size bowl.

☆ Stir the milk and vanilla together in a cup.

☆ Alternately add the milk-vanilla mixture and cocoa mixture to the creamed butter mixture, mixing until smooth between each addition.

☆ Grease a cookie sheet and drop on $1/4$ cup of batter at a time, making 20 cakes in all.

☆ Bake for 12 to 15 minutes.

☆ Cool the cakes completely while mixing the filling.

☆ To prepare the filling, chill a bowl and beaters in the freezer for at least 10 minutes.

☆ Pour the cream into the chilled bowl along with the vanilla and whip it until firm.

☆ Mix in the glazing sugar by hand.

☆ To assemble the Whoopee Pies, spoon the Chantilly cream onto the flat side of one cake and cover it with another cake, flat side down. Repeat until all the pies are made, then refrigerate them until serving.

Hint: Another option is to fill the pies with Raven's Rapture (see page 88) or a cream cheese or other icing.

DIVINATION DROPS

Yield: 1 dozen cupcakes

Foreseeing the pleasure others will derive from these delectable brownie cupcakes is unavoidable once you have tasted them yourself. Glazing them with Chocolate Shine (see page 55) adds a dimension of playfulness.

	P	C	F
3 ounces bittersweet chocolate	6	30	27
1$\frac{1}{2}$ sticks butter	1		132
3 eggs	21		21
1 teaspoon vanilla			
$\frac{1}{4}$ cup granulated sugar		100	
$\frac{1}{2}$ cup brown sugar		70	
$\frac{1}{4}$ cup tapioca flour		8	
$\frac{1}{4}$ cup rice flour	2	30	
$\frac{1}{4}$ cup soy flour	20	18	11
$\frac{1}{2}$ teaspoon salt			
2 teaspoons baking powder			
Total for 1 dozen cupcakes	**50**	**256**	**191**
Total per cupcake	**4**	**21**	**16**

☆ Preheat the oven to 350 degrees.

☆ Melt the chocolate and butter by microwaving it for 5 minutes on medium power or using a double boiler (or fill a large pot with water and then float a smaller pot on top, melting the chocolate and butter in the smaller pot). Stir occasionally until smooth. Let cool slightly.

☆ Blend the eggs and vanilla into the chocolate mixture.

☆ Combine the dry ingredients and stir into the chocolate mixture.

☆ Butter a muffin tin and ladle the batter into it, filling each cup approximately $\frac{2}{3}$ full.

☆ Bake for 30 to 40 minutes. When ready, the brownies will seem slightly undercooked.

FLYING CARPET ROLL

Yield: 1 jelly roll (16 slices)

This chocolate jelly roll, handed down from a cousin, is as magical as Prince Ahmed's legendary carpet. The moist but light sponge cake forms an airy counterpoint to the creamy filling, inviting new orbits of exploration. Whenever I bring this dessert to parties, people beg for the recipe—a chocolate lover's dream.

	P	C	F
Jelly roll:			
7 ounces bittersweet chocolate	14	70	63
4 tablespoons decaf coffee, brewed			
7 eggs, separated	49		49
3/4 cup sugar		75	
2 tablespoons cocoa	2	3	
Total for roll	65	148	112
Total per slice	4	9	7
Filling:			
9 tablespoons butter			99
3/4 cup glazing sugar		160	
3 ounces bittersweet chocolate	6	30	27
2 tablespoons decaf coffee, brewed (optional)			
2 eggs	14		14
Total filling	20	190	140
Total filling per slice	1	12	9
Total for filled roll	85	338	252
Total per slice	5	21	16

☆ Preheat the oven to 350 degrees.

☆ To prepare the jelly roll, cover a 10 x 15-inch jelly-roll pan with greased waxed paper.

☆ Melt the chocolate and coffee in a double boiler or microwave it at 50 percent power.

☆ Cool it slightly.

☆ Beat the egg yolks with $^1/_2$ cup of the sugar until peaks form.

☆ Add the chocolate and coffee mixture.

☆ In a separate bowl, beat the egg whites until peaks form, add $^1/_4$ cup sugar, and continue beating until stiff peaks form.

☆ Fold the egg white mixture into the chocolate and coffee mixture, spread it in the prepared pan, and bake for 18 to 20 minutes until firm.

☆ Remove the roll and cool for 5 minutes.

☆ Cover the roll with a damp towel and cool to room temperature.

☆ To prepare the filling, cream the butter and glazing sugar.

☆ Melt the chocolate with the coffee by microwaving it for 5 minutes on medium power or using a double boiler (or fill a large pot with water and then float a smaller pot on top, melting the chocolate and butter in the smaller pot). Stir until smooth and then cool.

☆ Add the butter mixture and blend until smooth.

☆ Blend in the eggs and set aside.

☆ To prepare the filled jelly roll, remove the towel and sprinkle the roll with the cocoa.

☆ Place a piece of waxed paper over the roll and reverse the pan, then remove the pan and the uppermost piece of waxed paper.

☆ Spread the filling on the jelly roll, roll gently, and decorate with shaved chocolate or glazing sugar, if desired.

Hint: If the rolling causes breaks, patch them with whipped cream or shaved chocolate.

HIDDEN TREASURE

Yield: 6 cakes

To penetrate Hidden Treasure's buttery, light chocolate exterior and come upon its warm liquid center is to indulge in the mystique of discovery. Prepared in individual servings, this elegant yet easy-to-make cake allows each guest a treasure of their own.

	P	C	F
1 stick butter			88
8 ounces bittersweet chocolate	12	84	72
4 large eggs	28		28
1 egg yolk			7
1 teaspoon vanilla			
1/4 teaspoon salt			
1/4 cup sugar		25	
1 tablespoon rice flour	1	10	
1 tablespoon tapioca flour		2	
Total for 6 cakes	**41**	**121**	**195**
Total per cake	**7**	**20**	**32**

☆ Preheat the oven to 400 degrees.

☆ Butter 6 ramekins and place them on a cookie sheet to catch any drippings during baking.

☆ Melt the butter and chocolate in a double boiler (or fill a large pot with water and then float a smaller pot on top, melting the butter and chocolate in the smaller pot) or microwave them in a glass bowl on medium power for 2 minutes, stirring and repeating until the mixture is smooth.

☆ With a mixer, beat the eggs, yolk, vanilla, salt, and sugar on high speed until the mixture turns very light in color and triples in volume.

☆ Sprinkle both flours onto the egg mixture and mix on low speed.

☆ Pour the melted chocolate mixture into the egg mixture.

☆ Using a wooden spoon or spatula, mix until the color is even, intermittently scraping the chocolate from the bottom.

☆ Pour the batter into the ramekins, bake for 10 to 12 minutes, and serve warm.

Hint: These cakes keep well in the refrigerator, where the mushy insides take on the consistency of a fudge brownie.

MARVELOUS MINIS
WITH GLUTEN

Yield: 3 dozen cupcakes

The first time I made a batch of these tiny chocolate cupcakes, I removed them from the oven just before my daughter came home from school and they were gone by dinnertime. At birthday parties they are even more elusive since their miniature size prompts children to reach out for more. Following are two recipes—one with gluten and one without.

	P	C	F
4 ounces bittersweet chocolate	8	40	36
1 stick butter			88
³/₄ cup sugar		75	
1 teaspoon vanilla			
4 eggs	28		28
3 tablespoons baking cocoa	3	9	
¹/₂ cup oat flour	5	27	3
¹/₄ cup rice flour	2	30	
¹/₄ cup tapioca flour		8	
¹/₈ teaspoon salt			
1 teaspoon xanthum gum			
Total for 3 dozen cupcakes	**46**	**189**	**155**
Total per cupcake	**1**	**5**	**4**

☆ Follow the directions on page 117.

MARVELOUS MINIS
WITHOUT GLUTEN

Yield: 3 dozen cupcakes

	P	C	F
4 ounces bittersweet chocolate	8	40	36
1 stick butter			88
³/₄ cup sugar		75	
1 teaspoon vanilla			
4 eggs	28		28
3 tablespoons baking cocoa	3	9	
¹/₂ cup rice flour	4	60	1
¹/₂ cup tapioca flour		16	
¹/₈ teaspoon salt			
2 teaspoons xanthum gum			
Total for 3 dozen cupcakes	**43**	**200**	**153**
Total per cupcake	**1**	**6**	**4**

Glaze: See Chocolate Shine (page 55).

☆ Preheat the oven to 350 degrees.

☆ Melt the butter and chocolate in a double boiler (or fill a large pot with water and then float a smaller pot on top, melting the butter and chocolate in the smaller pot) or microwave them in a glass bowl on medium power for 5 minutes, stirring and repeating until the mixture is smooth.

☆ Remove the mixture and stir in the sugar and vanilla.

☆ Stir in the eggs, one at a time.

☆ In a separate bowl, combine the cocoa, flours, salt, and xanthum gum.

☆ Stir the dry ingredients into the wet batter until it is smooth.

☆ Line a mini muffin tin with mini paper cups and fill them almost to the top with batter.

☆ Bake for 7 to 10 minutes.

(cont.)

☆ Remove the cupcakes from the tin and cool them completely.

☆ Repeat the process for the rest of the batter.

☆ Using a teaspoon, glaze the cupcakes with Chocolate Shine, if desired.

Hint: You may bake the cakes in standard muffin tins, increasing the baking time to 12 minutes (yield: $1^1/_2$ dozen cupcakes). Marvelous Minis without Gluten taste better when made a day in advance and stay moister if glazed.

MOONBEAM SUPREME

Yield: 1 cake (16 slices)

Cheesecake traditionalists are transfixed by this dessert's buttery nut crust and sweet thick cream filling. Even the most ardent of them do not miss the wheat-based, classic graham cracker crust.

	P	C	F
Filling:			
3 8-ounce packages cream cheese	48		240
4 eggs	28		28
6 tablespoons sugar		100	
1 teaspoon vanilla			
1/2 cup sour cream	4	5	24
Crust:			
1 1/2 cups nuts (3/4 cup walnuts	15	9	60
and 3/4 cup pecans)	3	15	51
1 stick butter	1		88
3 tablespoons sugar (optional)		25	
Topping:			
1/2 cup sour cream	4	5	24
2 tablespoons sugar		17	
Total for 16 slices	103	176	515
Total per slice	6	11	32

☆ Preheat the oven to 375 degrees.

☆ To make the filling, place the cream cheese, eggs, sugar, vanilla, and sour cream in a blender and process until smooth.

☆ To begin preparing the crust, chop the nuts finely.

☆ Melt the butter in a saucepan, then mix in the nuts and optional sugar.

☆ Spread the mixture in a 9-inch spring form pan, patting it with your fingers until smooth and even.

(cont.)

☆ Place the pan of nut crust on a jelly-roll pan and bake for 5 to 7 minutes. As the butter melts, it will drip through the spring form pan.

☆ Pour the blended cream cheese mixture over the nut crust and bake for another 25 minutes or until a cake tester comes out clean. The cake, having puffed up while baking, will sink when removed from the oven.

☆ In a small measuring cup or bowl, mix together ingredients for the topping and spread it over the cooled cake.

☆ Refrigerate, and serve chilled or at room temperature.

WICKED DARK DELIGHT

Yield: 1 torte (16 slices)

This fudgelike torte stimulates desires while simultaneously satiating them. Eating more than one piece is positively sinful.

	P	C	F
3 cups bittersweet chocolate chips	24	330	108
1 stick butter			88
5 eggs	35		35
Total for 16 slices	59	330	231
Total per slice	2	20	14

☆ Preheat the oven to 425 degrees.

☆ In a glass bowl, microwave the butter and chocolate on medium power for 5 minutes at a time, stirring until smooth. Or melt them in a double boiler (or fill a large pot with water and then float a smaller pot on top, melting the butter and chocolate in the smaller pot).

☆ Using a mixer, beat the eggs until slightly light and foamy.

☆ Pour the chocolate mixture into the eggs and fold until uniform.

☆ Butter a 9-inch spring form pan or 9-inch round cake pan and fill it with the batter.

☆ Bake for 10 to 15 minutes. Do not be concerned if the torte appears undercooked.

☆ When the torte has cooled, serve it topped with whipped cream or Raven's Rapture (see page 88) for an unforgettable experience.

Hint: To give this rich torte more mileage, you can divide the batter between 2 buttered pans or pie tins and bake for 5 to 8 minutes.

APPENDIX A

RESOURCES FOR HARD-TO-FIND INGREDIENTS

Your local health food store may stock these items or be willing to order them for you. If not, you can purchase them directly or request ordering information from the resources listed below.

All-Natural beef, lamb, chicken, pork, and jerky

> WolfeNeck Farms
> 184 Burnett Road
> Freeport, ME 04032
> 877-963-2333
> 207-865-4469
> E-mail: wnfarm@aol.com
> www.wolfesneckfarm.org
> (The definitions of "natural" versus "organic" change as requirements for organic labeling are altered. Currently, WolfeNeck's meats are considered "all natural.")

Antibiotic/nitrate-free pepperoni and Genoa salami

> Applegate Farms
> Branchbury, NJ 08876
> 800-587-5858
> www.applegatefarms.com

Buttermilk blend powder

> Saco Foods
> PO Box 620707
> Middleton, WI 57562-0707
> 800-373-7226
> E-mail: sacofoods@aol.com

Gluten-free baked goods without wheat, potatoes, or corn

Gillian's Foods, Inc.
55 Centre Street
Lynn, MA 01905
781-286-4095

Nitrate-free beef jerky

Vermont Beef Jerky Co.
RR 1, Box 50
Orleans, VT 05860
800-835-3759

Organic soy flour, oat flour, and brown rice flour

Fiddler's Green Farm
PO Box 254
Belfast, ME 04915
800-729-7935
E-mail: fiddler@mint.net
www.fiddlersgreenfarm.com

Organic turbino sugar, organic chocolate chips, organic butter, and organic vanilla

Northeast Coops
PO Box 8188
Brattleboro, VT 05304
800-321-2668
E-mail: newaccts@northeastcoop.com
www.northeastcoop.com

Organic turkey

The New Sharon Turkey Farm
209 Mile Hill Road
New Sharon, ME 04955
207-778-2889

Salt

The Salt and Grain Society
73 Fairway Drive
Asheville, NC 28805
800-867-7258
www.celtic-seasalt.com
(Also available are organic beans, organic almond butter, and many
other organic products.)

Tapioca flour

Ener-G-Foods, Inc.
PO Box 84487
Seattle, WA 98124-5787
800-331-5222

Bob's Red Mill
800-349-2173
www.bobsredmill.com

Xanthum gum

The Baker's Catalog
King Arthur Flour
PO Box 876
Norwich, VT 05055-0876
800-827-6836
www.KingArthurFlour.com
(This is also a source for good baking chocolate, although it is not
organic.)

Bob's Red Mill
800-349-2173
www.bobsredmill.com

MEASUREMENTS FOR INDIVIDUAL INGREDIENTS

Use the following protein/carbohydrate/fat ratios to create your own recipes for well-balanced meals. When converting measurements, remember that 3 tablespoons = $1/4$ cup.

	P	C	F
Chocolate			
1 ounce unsweetened chocolate	4	8	0
1 cup bittersweet chocolate	12	84	72
1 ounce bittersweet chocolate	2	10	19
1 cup bittersweet chocolate chips	8	110	36
1 tablespoon cocoa	1	3	0
Dairy and Eggs			
1 cup 2 percent milk	8	12	4
3 tablespoons buttermilk powder	4	10	0
1 cup dry milk	36	56	0
$2/3$ cup dry milk	24	37	0
1 cup light cream	6	8	46
1 cup heavy (whipping) cream	5	6	88
$1/2$ cup half and half	3	3	9
8 tablespoons butter (1 stick)	0	0	88
1 tablespoon butter	0	0	11
1 ounce cream cheese	2	0	10
$3/4$ cup cottage cheese, 4 percent fat	21	6	7
1 egg	7	0	7
3 egg whites	21	0	0
Flours			
1 cup tapioca flour	0	33	0
$1/2$ cup tapioca flour	0	16	0
1 cup rice flour	11	120	2
$1/2$ cup rice flour	5	60	1
1 cup soy flour	80	72	44

	P	C	F
1/2 cup soy flour	40	36	22
1 cup oat flour	10	54	6
1/2 cup oat flour	5	27	3

Meat and Fish

	P	C	F
1 pound boneless, skinless chicken breast	104	0	6
1 pound sirloin	144	0	50
4 ounces shrimp	23	0	1
4 ounces salmon	22	0	8

Nuts and Nut Butters

	P	C	F
1 cup pecans	7	17	70
1/4 cup pecans	1	5	17
1 cup walnuts	20	12	80
1/4 cup walnuts	5	3	20
1/4 cup peanut butter	12	10	24
1/4 cup almond butter	12	7	27

Oils

	P	C	F
1/4 cup coconut oil	0	0	42
1 tablespoon coconut oil	0	0	14
1/4 cup peanut oil	0	0	42
1 tablespoon peanut oil	0	0	14
1/4 cup olive oil	0	0	42
1 tablespoon olive oil	0	0	14
1 tablespoon sesame oil	0	0	14

Soy

	P	C	F
5 ounces tofu	25	6	13
1/2 cup TVP	23	14	0

Sugars

	P	C	F
1 cup granulated sugar	0	200	0
1/2 cup granulated sugar	0	100	0
1 tablespoon granulated sugar	0	8	0
1 cup brown sugar	0	141	0
1/2 cup brown sugar	0	70	0
1 tablespoon brown sugar	0	11	0

Appendix C

Glycemic Index

The glycemic index is determined by giving a person 50 grams of available carbohydrates from glucose or white bread, and seeing how much their blood sugar rises over the next few hours. The resulting blood sugar level is assigned a value of 100. Then all other foods tested are scaled accordingly. The following glycemic index is based on a white bread value of 100. To arrive at a glucose glycemic index for these foods, use the following conversion:

$$\text{Glucose glycemic index} = .7 \times \text{White bread glycemic index.}$$

Beverages	
Apple juice	58
Grapefruit juice	69
Milk, full-fat	39
Milk, skim	46
Milk, soy	43
Orange juice	78
Pineapple juice	66
Breads	
Bagel, white	103
Croissant	96
Doughnut	108
Hamburger bun	87
Mixed-grain bread	69
Oat bran bread	68
Pastry	84
Pita bread, white	82
Pizza, cheese	86

Cereals and Grains

Dairy

Fruits

Banana	77
Blackberries	Low
Blueberries	Low
Cantaloupe	92
Cherries	32
Dates	146
Grapefruit	36
Grapes	66
Jams and marmalades	70
Kiwi	75
Mango	80
Orange	63
Peach	60
Pear	53
Pineapple	94
Plum	55
Raisins	91
Raspberries	Low
Strawberries	45
Watermelon	103

Legumes

Baked beans, canned	69
Black beans	43
Chickpeas (Garbanzo beans)	47
Kidney beans	42
Kidney beans, canned	74
Lentils	41
Lima beans, baby, frozen	46
Mung beans	54
Peanuts	21
Pinto beans	55
Soybeans	25
Split peas, yellow, boiled	45

Pasta

Fettuccine 46
Macaroni 64
Spaghetti, protein enriched 38
Spaghetti, white 59
Vermicelli 50

Root Vegetables

Beets 91
Carrots 70
Parsnips 139
Potato, baked 121
Potato, white, boiled 80
Sweet potato 77
Taro 77
Yam 73

Sugars

Chocolate, sweetened 70
Fructose 32
Glucose 137
Honey 83
Lactose 65
Maltose 150
Sucrose 92

Vegetables

Alfalfa sprouts . . . . Low
Artichoke . . . . Low
Asparagus . . . . Low
Broccoli . . . . Low
Brussels sprouts . . . . Low

Cauliflower . . . . Low
Celery . . . . Low
Cucumber . . . . Low
Green bellpepper . . . . Low
Kale . . . . Low
Lettuce . . . . Low
Mushrooms . . . . Low
Onion . . . . Low
Peas, green 68
Snow peas . . . . Moderate
Spinach . . . . Low
Sweet corn 78
Swiss chard . . . . Low
Tomato . . . . Low
Zucchini . . . . Low

A Cauldron of Recommended Reading

Barnes, Broda, and Lawrence Galton. *Hypothyroidism: The Unsuspected Illness*. New York: Harper and Row, 1976.

Clark, Hulda. *The Cure for All Diseases*. Austin, TX: Forefront Technologies, 1993.

Enig, Mary. *Know Your Fats*. Silver Spring, MD: Bethesda Press, 2000.

Northrup, Christiane. *Wisdom of Menopause*. New York: Bantam Books, 2001.

Northrup, Christiane. *Woman's Bodies, Woman's Wisdom*. New York: Bantam Books, 1994.

Sears, Barry. *Enter the Zone*. New York: Harper Collins, 1995.

———*Mastering the Zone*. New York: Harper Collins, 1997.

———*The Soy Zone*. New York: Harper Collins, 2000.

Trowbridge, John. *The Yeast Syndrome*. New York: Bantam Books, 1986.

Index

Born and raised in Washington, DC, Eve Berman, DO, migrated to New England, where she found more cows and trees than people. After completing her osteopathic medical degree and postgraduate training, she opened a private practice in a small fishing village on the coast of Maine, where she currently resides with her husband, daughter, five cats, and perennial gardens. A specialist in Traditional Osteopathy with an extensive background in complementary modalities, Dr. Berman balances her time between patient care, teaching, home life, and creative cuisine for the body, mind, and spirit.

Order Form

Quantity		Amount
_____	*Culinary Potions: Eating Joyously with Food Allergies* ($16.95)	_____
	Sales tax of 5% for Maine residents	_____
	Shipping & handling (2–3 weeks delivery—$3.50 for first book, $1.00 for each additional book 5–7 days delivery—$5.00 for first book, $1.00 for each additional book)	_____
	Total amount enclosed	_____

Quantity discounts available.

Method of payment

❐ Check or money order enclosed
  (made payable to **Living Light Press** in US currency)
❐ MasterCard   ❐ VISA

Card #_____ Exp. date _____

Signature _____

Please contact your local bookstore or mail your order, together with your check, money order, or charge-card information, to:

- -

Living Light Press
PO Box 7266
Cape Porpoise, ME 04014
207-967-9936
www.culinarypotions.com

_____
Name

_____
Address

_____
City, State, Zip